BORN TO PLAY

Transcending Boredom into Play:
Supporting children to become captains of their own play adventures.

Anandé Ferreira

Transcending Boredom into Play:
Supporting children to become captains of their own play adventures.
Copyright © Anandé Ferreira 2021
Published by: PlayMore (Pty) Ltd
www.playmoreot.com

Editing and Proofreading by: Hannah van der Westhuizen
Book design and layout by: Kelly Lubbee | The Selula Journey
Cover design and book illustrations by: Jared Tromp
Printed and bound by: Print on Demand, Cape Town, South Africa

All rights reserved. No part of this publication may be reproduced, distributed, stored in a retrieval system or transmitted in any form or by any means, including photocopying, recording, or other electronic or mechanical methods, without the prior written permission of the publisher and copyright owner, except in the case of brief quotations embodied in critical reviews and certain non-commercial uses permitted by copyright law.

For permission requests please email the publisher, subject line: *'Born to Play Permissions'* at admin@playmoreot.com.

This book is for educational or informational purposes only and is not intended to act as a substitute for medical advice or treatment. Any person with a condition requiring medical attention should consult a medical practitioner or therapist. The advice and strategies found within may not be suitable for every situation. The author and publisher shall not be held liable or responsible for any loss or damage allegedly resulting from any information or suggestion in the book. While the author made every attempt to provide accurate internet addresses at the time of the publication, the author and publisher will not assume any responsibility for changes that occur after publication. Furthermore, the author and publisher does not have any control over and does not assume any responsibility for third-party websites or their content.

Paperback ISBN 978-0-620-92613-3
eBook ISBN 978-0-620-92614-0

To my husband Ryan, for your ongoing support, love and encouragement throughout this process ... in lockdown, during a pandemic. I would still be busy writing if it wasn't for you, 'For my ally is the Force, and a powerful ally it is.' – Yoda
(Jip, a Star Wars quote just for you)

To my parents for nurturing my playful nature and for providing me with a childhood that cherished play in all its forms, including Roftie. You have made it possible for me to follow my dreams.

To Rey, the best lockdown buddy.

To Maré, for the bus ride to Madison and the many talks since then #playmore.

To the children and families that I have worked alongside with over the years.

Thank you all!

TABLE OF CONTENTS

About the author	7
Introduction	8
Chapter 1: In Pursuit of Play	12
A closer look at play	14
Play and non-play	17
Play structures	17
Decline of free play	24
Play Development	25
• Birth to two years old	25
• Two to four years old	28
• Four to six years old	29
Social Play Stages	31
• Unoccupied play stage	31
• Solitary play stage	31
• Onlooker play stage	32
• Parallel play stage	33
• Associative play stage	33
• Cooperative or collaborative play stage	34
Play Categories	35
• Physical and sensory play	35
• Language play	39
• Exploratory play	39
• Constructive play	40
• Fantasy play	40
• Social play	40

Chapter 2: The Play Context — 44
The play context — 46
Caregivers — 47
- Play styles — 49

Playmates — 52
The physical and sensory play environment — 56
Screen time — 58
Policy and curriculums — 64

Chapter 3: The Child at Play — 68
The child at play — 70
Playfulness — 71
Play interests — 72
Developmental skills — 77
Sensory needs — 78

Chapter 4: Playful Ways — 92
Playful ways — 94
The role of the caregiver in play — 94
Developmental considerations and play stages — 97
Play interest considerations — 101
Play spaces and play prompts — 106
Supporting free play engagement — 116
- My child always wants me to play with them — 116
- The PlayMore here and near dance — 116
- How do I join my child's play? — 118
- Don't take the fun out of free play — 118
- My child can't choose what to play — 119
- "I'm bored" - Jump start play — 119
- How do I support risky play? — 124

Chapter 5: Play for All — 132
Play for all — 134

Conclusion — 135
Additional Acknowledgements — 137
References — 138

ABOUT THE AUTHOR

Anandé Ferreira

My love of play was nurtured from a young age, which I believe set me on the journey through my studies, research and clinical practice, cultivating a special interest in play and playfulness.

My childhood was filled with playful opportunities, including my imaginary horse friend. Initially, the stories my parents told me of their role in our adventures were quite funny, but over time, what stood out more was the way my parents nurtured my playful nature and provided me with an environment, both at home and out and about, that cherished play in all its forms.

After a period of wonderful play adventures, my imaginary friend eventually went off on his own adventures, but you'll find him in the PlayMore logo. To me, he is a symbol of the joy that play can bring, the connection and bonding between caregivers and children, exploration, learning and development that all form part of the magic of free play.

Outside of the hours spent play training with my aforementioned imaginary horse, I trained in a more academic and professional sense as a paediatric occupational therapist. I am now in private practice, with a special interest in playfulness and a certification in sensory integration therapy, obtained in 2016 (SAISI).

Upon completion of my Masters' degree in 2016, focused on playfulness, I presented my research at the World Federation of Occupational Therapists Congress in 2018 and was published in the Occupational Therapy International Journal in 2018. I am a guest lecturer in play assessments, playfulness and play interventions in the Occupational Therapy Department at the University of Cape Town. I run continued professional development workshops and courses for qualified occupational therapists, focused on the aforementioned topics. I adore immersing myself in the world of play.

Recognising the critical role of caregivers in their child's play, development and learning, I want to support and empower caregivers with knowledge and practical strategies to help children to reach their full potential. In working towards this objective, I created the PlayMore Online Platform in 2019, which supports caregivers and children in creating more playful engagement in today's ever-changing, fast-paced world.

INTRODUCTION

I started writing this book a few days into January 2020, when COVID-19 was merely the start of an event, a pandemic that would eventually affect us all. I find myself completing this book under lockdown, which has continued far longer than we initially thought, a concept that would have seemed so strange and surreal had anyone described it to me in early January.

Lockdown placed a burden on many parents, who found themselves in multiple roles: parent, worker, teacher and, for some, full-time playmate as well. The pressure to *school* and to *occupy* young children came to light through social media observations and the panicked messages I received, as concerned parents tried to navigate and manage these various roles.

Many structured, adult-led activities would be labelled as #play and #fun by caregivers during this time. It only took a quick glance at their pictured toddler's face, who had suddenly been enrolled in a new curriculum, to know that it was in fact not #play and certainly not #fun. I noted an increase in the number of young children pictured in adult-led, structured activities that were misrepresented, or perhaps misunderstood by caregivers, as 'play'. This was not play.

I feared that competitive parenting and comparisons on social media had placed unrealistic expectations on many children who were not developmentally ready for the tasks that were expected of them.

Soon after, came e-learning schedules and Zoom calls put together by some preschools and early years programmes, which, in some cases, involved hours of seated, sedentary learning and worksheets. I understand that circumstances required many of these preschools and early years programmes to become inventive, to adapt. However, how much of this was done at the expense of the children that the programmes were meant to nurture in the first place? How much of this was done to please a consumer-driven approach to early years education and parental beliefs that *earlier is better* without aligning developmental norms with activity expectations? How much of this was done to keep children busy, to occupy them, so that adults could get on with their tasks, rather than considering what would be best for children's wellbeing and development?

In a podcast interview I had done in February 2020, I mentioned that we, as a society, need to learn to trust in play again. I saw this repeatedly throughout lockdown. Some parents would proudly post their two-, three- and four-year olds completing, or rather attempting to complete, what felt to me, on the other side of my screen, to be a never-ending flow of structured activities and worksheets, in a fear response that they may fall behind their peers.

Again, the message was pushing early writing, literacy and numeracy skills onto very young children who do not necessarily have the developmental building blocks to gain and learn from those structured activities and worksheets. Furthermore, the opportunity cost of missing out on precious play years and play adventures can have detrimental effects on their development and wellbeing.

> "The majority of children play less than previous generations, yet more is expected of them at earlier and earlier ages."

This did not sit comfortably with me. I felt sorrow for children missing out on the magic of play adventures, at a time when they so desperately needed the medium of play for their own health and wellbeing. I felt sorrow for caregivers who placed their trust in an early rush towards academic skills, perhaps not fully understanding the impact this can have on their children. I felt sorrow for early years educators who felt they had no choice but to overshadow the importance of play in an attempt to satisfy parental demands or to comply with a (often unrealistic) curriculum with which they do not necessarily agree. I felt sorrow in observing a larger societal distrust of play and a misrepresentation of what constitutes play.

The majority of children play less than previous generations, yet more is expected of them at earlier and earlier ages: to sit for longer periods without an opportunity to strengthen their bodies for that very expectation, to write earlier without an opportunity to strengthen their hands and develop the very hand skills required for that task and to engage in maths and reading without the necessary developmental building blocks and concrete experiences in place. This is the plight of the indoor generation.

You might wonder, well, why don't children simply play more then? It depends. It depends on the child and it depends on their surrounding play context. This book is for the caregiver who seeks a deeper understanding of how to nurture play and how to create an environment that supports playful engagement. This book aims to empower you, as a caregiver, to understand the difference between play and non-play and to reflect on factors impacting your child's play. It also includes how-to strategies to set you on a more playful path.

In the following chapters, 1-4, you will find a 'Pause to Play' reflection-style workbook that aims to assist you in the process of understanding and unpacking the contextual and child-related factors that are most relevant to you and your family unit and the strategies that may be best suited to your particular context. I do not believe in a one golden-rule approach. Every child and every family are unique. Let's not try to keep up with the Joneses or their elaborate and picture-perfect social media account.

This book, written through the lens of my occupational therapy experience, is the culmination of my research, clinical experience, talks, workshops, posts, articles and online videos.

Shall we start our play adventure?

"Play is a paradox because it both is
and is not what it appears to be."

- Sutton Smith, 2007, p.1

CHAPTER ONE

IN PURSUIT OF PLAY

A CLOSER LOOK AT PLAY

Sutton-Smith (1997) and Bundy (2002) described play as a transaction between an individual and the environment. I value this description of play, as it brings to light the various factors that contribute to a playful engagement. I have found this quite apt in the current milieu. In my opinion, the pandemic brought to the foreground many environmental and contextual factors that have impacted on play for a long period of time.

Caregivers reached out to me when the initial hard lockdown commenced, raising concerns that they had observed that their children struggled to play independently and had difficulty in occupying themselves. It can be hard to be good at something that you rarely have the time and the opportunity to do... even play.

Contextual factors, such as overscheduling of children with extra murals, competitive parenting, parental beliefs around play and learning (with some parents viewing play as nonsense and less important than, often developmentally inappropriate, structured learning activities), longer school days with fewer play breaks and screens, impact on children's time and opportunity to play. So yes, play can be hard (or, sadly, missing altogether) when it is not consciously supported and celebrated by the adults in a child's life. If a child has limited opportunities for play at school and at home, where can they engage in deep, uninterrupted free play?

In contrast, we may have a child with various play opportunities and a supportive play context who struggles to give and read play cues with their peers, struggles to enter an abstract, imaginary world or is unable to engage in unstructured free play without ideas from their caregivers.

At times, we may have both an environment (or rather a play context) that does not effectively support play and a child with play needs that limit the overall play engagement.

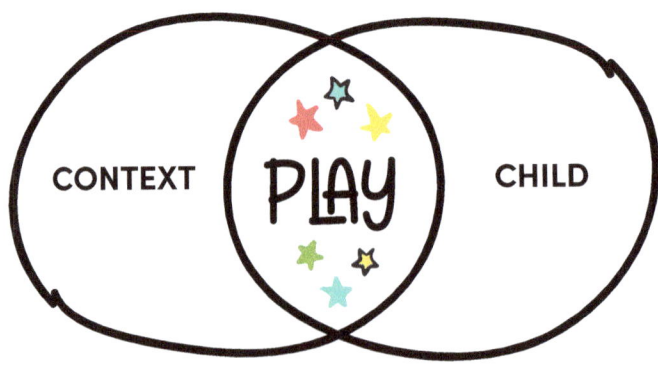

Figure 1: The Play Transaction

The context does not only refer to the physical, built environment, i.e. how large or small it is, the play prompts available, or the lack thereof, but also includes the consideration of caregivers and playmates. Do caregivers create a safe and nurturing environment? Do caregivers know how to support and guide play, and not simply direct play? Does the adult agenda or the right way to play mentality impact on play? How supportive and inclusive are playmates in the various contexts?

Therefore, the environment component refers to external environmental or contextual factors, including physical, sensory and socio-emotional factors, and broader economic, political and social factors that may either support or inhibit play.

The child component refers to a child's temperament, developmental and cognitive skills, play skills and playfulness and, I would also like to further include their individual sensory needs as part of the play transaction. The child components refer to the skills (or needs) a child would bring to the play transaction.

We need to look at both the child and contextual components of play, as both are needed for that magical play engagement to occur. Before discussing these components in more detail, let's first take a look at play.

Play is not easily defined. In Sutton-Smith's book, *The Ambiguity of Play*, he outlined seven different views about play and its importance. Depending on your lens, you may have different values or beliefs about play than another person. Therefore, different contexts may have different play values.

The first view of play focuses on the important contribution play makes to child development and that play, similar to child development, is believed to progress through stages.

> Free play is NOT providing a child with an exact activity, with exact instructions and expecting an exact outcome. That is an activity.

This view focuses on the importance of play in contributing to physical, socio-emotional and cognitive development, rather than children engaging in play for fun or enjoyment. In other words, it focuses on what play can do to further a child's skillset.

Play is further described as a demonstration and experience of power, during play engagements and also over external objects. A different understanding of play is as an expression of identity, bonding, culture and traditions, through engaging in rituals and play activities that have been passed down from generation to generation. Another perspective describes the relationship between play and imagination through autonomy, a sense of control and creative exploration of the self and the surrounding environment and its materials.

Play has also been viewed with a focus on satisfaction, joy, fun and relaxation, with a player engaging in self-chosen activities for the purpose of building an inner identity. This viewpoint focuses on the self, with the flow of experience, as described by Csikszentmihalysis (and yes, I also cannot read that name aloud) tying into this view and experience of play. The final viewpoint describes play, in itself, as frivolous and without a particular purpose or goal.

A summary of Sutton-Smith's conclusions regarding play is that play holds both a broad and a narrow definition. It can include active and passive forms, it applies to humans and animals, children and adults and it can be a momentary or a prolonged experience. Play, in the eye of its beholder, has been shaped by context and cultural values.

I think it is necessary for caregivers to take a conscious step to reflect on their view of play and what has contributed, knowingly or unknowingly, to the belief you may hold about play. It may be a blend of motives or values. Furthermore, to realise that during free play, your child's experience and motivation to play may not always align with the belief you hold of or importance you assign to play. Your child may be playing as a means to soothe and regulate, while you may view the play engagement as important for developing their fine motor skills. The same play engagement can hold different values for different players. Unfortunately, the child's experience of play does not always seem to be widely respected.

Research has demonstrated that caregivers who believe that play is responsible for development and learning, will more likely play with their child and support playful engagement within the home context. However, to me, it seems that the societal view of what constitutes play has mostly (but not for all individuals) become skewed. In the next section we will unpack the different structures of play and consider what constitutes play and non-play.

> "Play is, first and foremost, an expression of freedom. It is what one wants to do as opposed to what one is obliged to do."
>
> - Peter Gray, 2013, p. 141

PLAY AND NON-PLAY

> *"Play, say the experts, inspires imagination and invention, helping children attain positive emotions and control negative ones."*
>
> – Howard Chudacoff, 2007, p. 1

The skewed view, by some, of what constitutes play, along with the pressure and rush towards early achievement of pre-academic and academic skills, appear to have contributed to the misrepresentation and labelling of structured activities as play. In this process, it seems that society at large has either forgotten what play is, attempted to soften the amount of adult-led and structured activities by labelling them as play or does not understand the value and importance of play. Whatever the reason, I think it is critical that caregivers, whether parents at home or early year educators, reflect on their understanding of activity versus play, i.e. what constitutes play and non-play.

Let's first look at the most agreed-upon features of play:
- It is **self-chosen** by the child.
- The child is **intrinsically motivated**.
- The motivation is the **enjoyment and process** of play, rather than a specific end result or award.

Other features that have often been mentioned by scholars and researchers include:
- Play requires **engagement** on the part of the player.
- It is **spontaneous**.
- It includes **non-literality** (in other words, it is marked off from reality in some way and is not restricted by a specific set of rules or boundaries).

PLAY STRUCTURES

With these features in mind let us look at the differences between adult-led, guided and free play.

In adult-led play, which I will refer to as adult-led activity, or simply activity, activities have a specific goal, outcome or set of rules associated with them. Adult-led activities are organised or led by an adult who directs how, when, with what and for how long the child engages in the particular activity, with an expected outcome in mind, of course. This is often product driven, as children replicate an example or follow very specific, and often restrictive, instructions. Children are often provided with an adult-made end product, rather than being provided with books and materials that can inspire them to create their vision of the particular theme, and their end results are often corrected or fixed by an adult to be more in line with the example.

A lack of focus on freedom and process during the early years limits children's ability to think creatively, to explore and to engage in critical problem solving, to only name a few skills for now. It can contribute to a robotic, recipe following, 'Am I doing it right?', 'Can someone else help me to do it right?' or 'Can someone else do it for me?' generation.

This type of adult-led activity falls towards non-play.

Process art prioritises the creative exploration of media. It is open ended, and the end product will represent a unique, original and child-driven motivation and thought process.

Product art is close ended and requires the step-by-step exact replication of an adult-made model.

Guided play sees adults setting up and scaffolding play opportunities for children. The Vygotsky concept, *The Zone of Proximal Development*, can be applied within this play structure. This refers to an area of competence that a child can access with the assistance or guidance of an adult, older peer or in collaboration with a group of peers. Guided play requires a caregiver to use strategies and principles to provide subtle guidance to shape the process and behaviours along the way, all while following the child's lead. Child agency is a critical part of guided play. Guided play requires skill on the part of the caregiver.

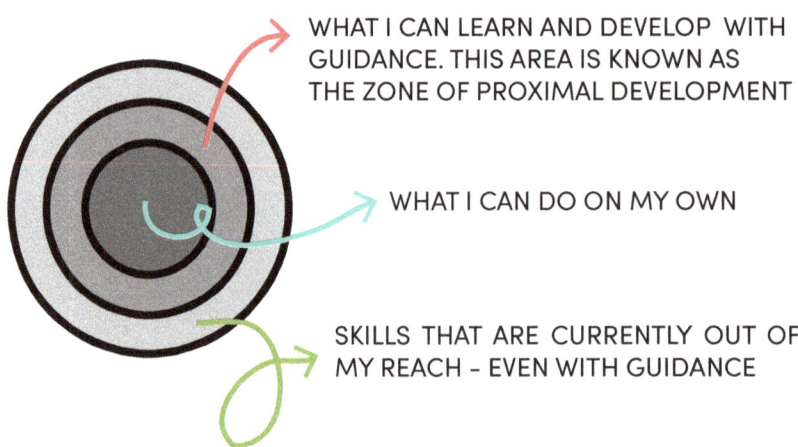

Figure 2 Illustration of The Zone of Proximal Development – Vygotsky (1978)

Free play characteristics are that play is child directed, intrinsically motivated, spontaneous, not limited by a certain set of directives, not necessarily reality bound and fuelled by the enjoyment of the process itself. Children can create, direct and adapt play scripts and the surrounding play milieu, alone or with a playmate, as they engage in their play adventure. My view of free play is based on Anita Bundy's model of playfulness, which is described in more detail below.

These three play structures, adult-led activity, guided play and play, can be seen on a continuum ranging from non-play to play, with adult-led activity falling towards non-play, guided play in the centre (dependent on the skill level of the caregiver involved) and free play falling towards play.

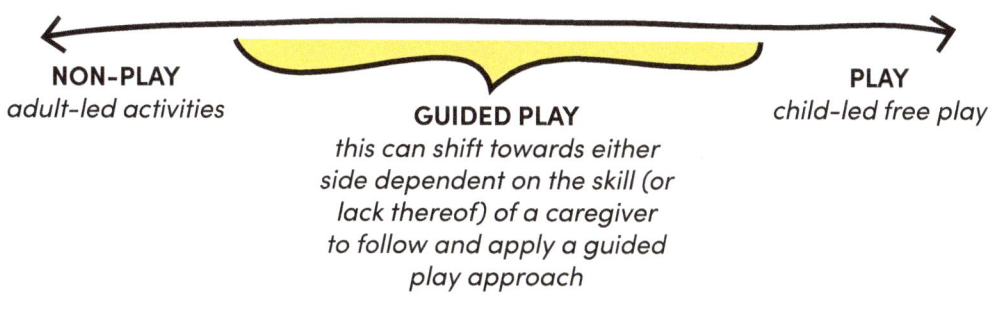

Figure 3: Play Continuum 1
Adapted from Skard and Bundy (2008); Pyle and Daniels (2017)

Skard and Bundy (2008) described a model of playfulness that consists of the following four elements: intrinsic motivation, internal control, ability to suspend reality and framing.

Intrinsic motivation refers to a child's willingness to engage in play, as observed through the process and enjoyment of engaging in play itself, not necessarily to achieve a particular product or because someone told them to do so. Intrinsic motivation speaks to a child's inner drive to engage in play and provides insight into their play interest/s.

Internal control involves a child's independent decision making with regard to their play choices. This doesn't mean they have control over all aspects, if you are concerned about this, but rather that they have freedom to choose within options presented to them in the play space. In other words, they have control over what to play, how to play, where to play and, at times, with whom to play. Internal control allows them to make choices that are in line with their current intrinsic motivation to play. As part of internal control, we can differentiate between individual and shared control. The latter refers to a child choosing to join and play a game that their peers are playing, sharing control within the play engagement. Bundy (2002) mentioned that, '(f)eeling physically and emotionally safe is the most basic aspect of internal control' (p. 231). In order for a child to fully immerse themselves in play, they need to feel safe within their surrounding environment (this does not take away from healthy risky play, which we will discuss later). Here, we consider the importance of connection, of feeling physically and emotionally safe and having basic human needs met.

Freedom to suspend reality refers to a child's ability to pretend. In some instances of fantasy play, they may use an object as it was intended, as part of their play script, such as using a cup as a cup, or they may disregard its properties and characteristics and pretend that it serves a different purpose, such as turning it into a telescope. Furthermore, pretense play allows them to try out, practice and/or experience roles or situations without necessarily experiencing the real-life consequences. The play milieu eases the consequences by offering a safe space to process and engage.

Framing refers to the ability to appropriately give, read and respond to play cues.

A child who is internally motivated and chooses their own play engagement is deemed more playful, and their play will fall towards the right-hand side of Figure 3. In contrast, a child who engages in play for an extrinsic reward and does not choose the play activity, for example, a caregiver who asks, 'Please play with this puzzle for 10 minutes, and then you can watch YouTube videos,' will fall towards non-play.

Free play is NOT providing a child with an exact activity, with exact instructions and expecting an exact outcome. That is an activity. Children who are engaging solely in structured activities are missing out on the various benefits of play. Benefits, which, in my opinion, cannot be replicated or replaced by giving a child more structured activities.

Why do I feel it is important for caregivers to distinguish between non-play and play? I think it is necessary for us to acknowledge that some children's preschool curriculum or time at home may be spent engaged in activities, not play. Furthermore, by adding more non-play activities to a child's day, while reducing or removing their play opportunities, also removes their time to regulate, reset, explore, discover, learn and enjoy their own play interests. This time is important for their development, health and wellbeing.

Free play provides children with the opportunity to work on various developmental areas and skills, such as problem solving, reasoning, creativity, flexible thinking, initiative and grit, self-regulation skills, working memory, sustained focus, **STEAM** skills and physicality. It can also provide them with an opportunity to have some quiet time to soothe and regulate themselves. Free play with a playmate can further see children develop various socio-emotional skills, including self-expression, negotiation, compromise, collaboration, perspective taking and empathy. Important skills for the future... wouldn't you say?

The addition of the A, to expand STEM to STEAM skills, refers to the Arts. This includes the creative process and ingenuity as part of discovery and problem solving. Therefore, the acronym refers to:

There are some benefits to adult-led activities, before you think I am all about the cons. It allows for higher risk activities, such as teaching children how to use new equipment in the kitchen. It also allows the opportunity to learn a new skill or concept. However, there are studies that have indicated that guided play is more beneficial and effective for young children in learning new concepts. Unfortunately, the adult to child ratio in most play or preschool contexts impacts on whether guided play can take place in a classroom. This has also partially contributed to direct instruction and adult-led activities dominating in many (but not all) early years learning environments.

An unfortunate shift in many, please hear me say many, and not all, home contexts and schooling curriculums is an earlier push towards pre-academic and academic skills when children are not yet developmentally ready. For example, letter and number formation are introduced at earlier and earlier stages when children have not yet acquired the developmental building blocks for these tasks. Adult-led activities are not always effective and can be limited in what they can teach a child and, as mentioned earlier, often focus on a very specific or limited learning outcome. Yes, some structured activities may be experienced as fun, depending on the child and their interests, but if we reflect again on the play features that would make it a fun activity, not play.

In contrast, guided play's associated benefits, IF the adult is skilled in guiding play, is a love of learning. Guided play balances the child's autonomy and intrinsic motivations with adult guidance. Therefore, the adult can meet the child at their level and scaffold their activities to ensure success, using the Vygotsky zone of proximal development concept, as mentioned earlier. If done with the correct strategies and cues, this approach can be more effective at teaching young children new concepts than direct instruction. Furthermore, as guided play taps into a child's agency, it can share similar benefits to those mentioned earlier in free play skills.

The limitations of guided play include an adult's skill in meeting the child at their level, allowing autonomy and following the child's lead with open-ended questions and inquiry. Guided play relies on a smaller adult to child ratio and smaller groups than we see in many schooling systems and programmes. If the ratio is too big, and the adult is not able to appropriately scaffold, ask open-ended questions and guide the process, it can shift towards either end of the non-play to play continuum. It can shift towards free play if an adult does not have the time to engage and guide the children appropriately, or it can shift to adult-led activity if they start setting up stations that children should complete in a particular time and with particular rules, without child agency coming into the equation.

With regard to free play, I want to touch on open-ended and goal-directed play as part of this play structure. Open-ended play prioritises spontaneity, fun and creativity. It is all about the journey and the process of play, with no particular destination in mind. An astronaut can go to the princess' tea party after their trip to the moon, save a lion on the way and bring it with them.

Open-ended play does not refer to close-ended toys, such as a child who chooses to complete a puzzle in their own time, of their own accord. In these instances, the child is goal-directed, following a particular recipe or set of rules, but is not being told to do so. In other words, free play can include both open-ended and goal-directed play, with the critical difference being that, in both instances, it is completely self-chosen, intrinsically motivated and spontaneous.

Therefore, independent free play occurs when children choose what to engage in, for how long to engage in it and how to direct their own play, with no, or minimal, adult interference. This tilts the play transaction towards play. At times, children may choose to include skills that they find difficult or skills they want to practice without an audience, in their own time, at their own pace and without being rewarded or told to do so.

Young children's imitation and keen observation skills can be brought into their free play as they attempt to learn and master new skills through self-chosen, intrinsically motivated play choices. Yes, it may take longer to succeed than with the assistance of an adult or playmates, but through trial and error, grit and persistence, we may hear a triumphant, 'I did it!'.

If we consider the features of play previously mentioned, although both goal-directed and open-ended play can fall under free play, in my opinion, open-ended play taps into more features of play. Therefore, I have placed it on the right-hand side of Figure 4, towards the end of play, when compared with goal-directed play.

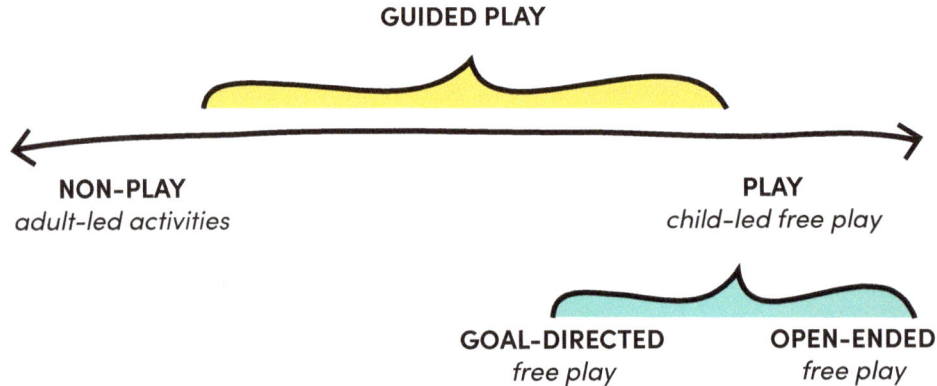

Figure 4: Play Continuum 2
Adapted from Skard and Bundy (2008); Pyle and Daniels (2017)

Adult-led activity and free play may, at times, include similar choices, such as puzzles, drawing or painting. However, the circumstances surrounding the engagement are where the difference lies. In free play, there is internal control. The child is intrinsically motivated and chooses to do the activity. They can stop at any time, or they can leave the activity and start something else and return to it later if they would like.

Now, you probably didn't see this coming, but free play can have limitations. An important consideration with regards to free play is whether the play setting or play space is well equipped with a variety of play materials that tap into various play categories. If not, it may lead to restricted play choices, contributing to some developmental skills being less well developed than others. Furthermore, some children may avoid play categories that are challenging for them, resulting in possible developmental gaps forming.

If we compare a baby who is frequently placed in containers (eg. car seats, jumpers, walkers, etc.) with limited opportunities to explore their body movements, senses and the world around them, to a baby with a safe and stimulating 'yes' space (covered later in Chapter 4: *Playful Ways*) who can manoeuvre, play and explore freely, the surrounding play context will impact on the rate and acquisition of skills through play, such as sitting, crawling and walking.

Children are naturally curious and keen explorers, little scientists who are eagerly testing and making discoveries along the way. A hypothesis can't be tested only once, and repetition allows children to see if they get the same result each time. If I drop a ball, it bounces, but if I drop playdough or food, it sticks to the floor – much to our caregivers' dismay. Repetition allows children to observe differences in outcomes and to compare, categorise and learn from their experiences. Repetition is required, not only to build strong pathways in the brain, but also because the very process of making discoveries brings joy and pleasure. And then ... because it was fun, we want to do it all over again! This helps to build their confidence as they learn and master various skills through play.

A balance of free play and guided play opportunities for young children can provide joy, freedom, developmental skill acquisition and learning through play. For parents, early years educators, au pairs and other caregivers, I hope this section will allow you to reflect on the approach to play that is most used in your home or preschool environment. Is there a balance between adult led or, preferably, guided play and free play opportunities? Was the play you deemed part of the programme or day free play, or does it fall more towards non-play? This reflection is important in the process of introducing or creating time and opportunity for play where it has been missing.

THE DECLINE OF FREE PLAY

Over the past years, or rather decades, as Howard Chudacoff explores and examines in his book, *Children at Play,* along with other recent research studies, we have seen shifts in play trends due to various contextual factors.

These include:
- Caregiver concerns around crime and safety.
- Less availability of and access to safe outdoor play environments.
- Changes to school hours, e.g. longer school days and shortened breaks.
- Changes to school curriculums and policies, which add to pre-academic and academic pressures, due to poor or limited consultation with early childhood educators and specialists.
- More dual income families.
- Increased time spent traveling between schools, activities and places of work (certainly prior to lockdown).
- Competitive parenting or fear of the future, with concerns around academic achievement and performance in various extra murals contributing to an increase in time spent in structured, organised activities, and play being deemed less important.
- An increase in screen time.

Each family unit may have different factors contributing to the decline in, or lack of, free play within their context. It is not only the lack of play but also the inability to engage in play that has been a growing concern. For these reasons, **I believe it is not enough to simply tell caregivers that children should 'just play more', as I feel this has led to many caregivers further serving the 'I'm bored' culture with activities, rather than nurturing the 'I'm bored' space.**

For many caregivers, children and families, the lack of free play is owing to the contextual and children components in Figure 1 not overlapping. It is not always a simple fix to *just play more*. Therefore, it is important for you, as a caregiver, to reflect and start to understand where your child's play needs lie. Is it the play space, the play prompts, the way you as a caregiver scaffold and cue play or perhaps child factors? This is what we will explore in this book to empower you and your child to unlock more play.

The important role of play in a child's life is well documented, and I believe it is important to provide caregivers and children with opportunities to play within their context. Play deprivation can have a negative impact on physical, cognitive and socio-emotional development, and it is therefore critical that we continue to bring play to the foreground.

I would like to end this section with this quote from Peter Gray, a favourite of mine:

'Perhaps play would be more respected if we called it something like "self-motivated practice of life skills", but that would remove the light-heartedness from it and thereby reduce its effectiveness. So, we are stuck with the paradox. We must accept play's triviality in order to realize its profundity.' - *Peter Gray, 2013, p. 156*

PLAY DEVELOPMENT

Birth to two years old

The birth to two years age group marks a period of exceptional growth and development, with many firsts and milestones occurring with the help of stimulation, nurturing bonds and safe environments.

This period focuses on the exploration of senses, body movements, objects and the environment surrounding the child. They are keen observers and imitators. They enjoy play opportunities that allow for practice and repetition of new motor skills and simple problem solving.

Body language, gestures and facial expressions form part of the earliest play cues and the beautiful back-and-forth communication that can occur between a caregiver and an infant.

The first five months is a period focused on exploring senses, body parts and body movements. From about five or six months infants will develop more of an interest in objects and toys, rather than simply grasping at them.

During the early months, infants initiate play rather than following a caregivers' play cues. Infants may imitate a caregiver or sibling's action, which, if picked up on, can turn into a back-and-forth play exchange or *serve and return*, as described by The Center on the Developing Child, Harvard University.

Initially, infants' play cues might not be very apparent to caregivers, especially before infants develop the ability to point and move closer to objects. However, play cues can include shaking or banging objects, feeling different textures on a mat or attempting to kick and pull suspended items. In these early play moments, a caregiver can already tune in, acknowledge and imitate what baby is doing and expand on the play action. Their play cues will continue to strengthen and expand with body language and verbal language over time.

> **tip!**
>
> Cues that indicate that baby is ready to play include cooing, making eye contact, turning toward their caregivers' voice and smooth, relaxed body movements. However, a baby turning away, avoiding eye contact, fussing and/or exhibiting jerky movement indicates that they are not ready or interested.

These earlier play moments rely heavily on facial expressions and social gaze, which is why screens can interfere greatly in this process. Babies need three-dimensional, real-life experiences and a present caregiver, not a screen. Infants use their caregiver's gaze and eye contact to guide their social interactions, such as responding to their caregiver's eye contact with a smile. By ten months of age, the social gaze develops further, and the baby is able to look at their caregiver, notice that the caregiver is looking at a particular object and then follow their gaze to look at the same object. This shared visual attention is important for social learning and developing communication.

The reverse can also happen, where baby may look at the object in their hand, look up at their caregiver and back at the toy, as a cue to say, 'Hey, look over here at what I'm doing,' as they initiate joint attention. This requires an attentive and present caregiver during an infant's quiet alert moments.

Once they are more mobile and their hand manipulation continues to develop, we see instances of infants showing or passing an object while observing their caregiver. This is where caregivers can build on a back-and-forth play exchange by doing something with the object. Let's say they pass you a ball and you bounce it, or a rattle and you shake it. Then you hand the item back to them. They may imitate you and expand on the back-and-forth exchange, or they might choose a new item altogether. These instances build on and expand their repertoire through their keen observation and imitation skills.

Tune in to an infant turning their body or face away as a sign that they are becoming overstimulated and then allow for independent exploration of the item. In these moments, reduce the amount of sensory input, for example commenting on or imitating every action. Simply be there and allow for independent exploration. As we will discuss later, as part of the caregiver role in free play, this is the earliest form of a 'here and near dance'. During these baby play moments, we allow and start developing their capacity for independent free play.

Intense Play Interests

Intense Play Interests: From dinosaurs, balls and dolls to trains and transport.
A study by DeLoache, Simcock and Macari (2007) found that nearly a third of the children in their study had an intense play interest. These intense play interests were more common in young boys, with an average age of emergence of a particular intense interest of 18 months. The intense play interest lasted anywhere between six and 36 months, with an average duration of 22 months. Alexander et al. (2008) found that, for some children, an intense play interest could last until six years of age, but diminished as children entered formal schooling, while some carried their passions into adulthood, from hobbies to career choices.
You may be wondering, what are the benefits of intense interests? Studies have found a positive association between intense play interests and sustained focus, perseverance, complex thinking, language skills, creativity and processing skills.

Between 12 and 18 months, toddlers will start pointing to and gesturing at objects with more intent and may be able to name a favourite toy or item, allowing for play cues to become more apparent to caregivers. We want to continue to expand on their free play capacity by following their lead and the flow of their play. Their attention spans are still developing. Initially we may have a short back-and-forth play exchange of one or two play actions, lasting one to two minutes, to eventually being able to play with a single object, or two, independently for a few additional minutes.

From about 12 to 18 months onwards, infants will start displaying simple pretend actions, particularly relating to events in their routine with which they are familiar. These may include pretending to feed someone else, initially you, a sibling or even the dog and then moving onto inanimate objects, such as feeding a doll. Pretend actions are often first focused on people or animals before inanimate objects, while also using real household objects as the pretend object during the play action, such as the spoon they were using to feed themselves.

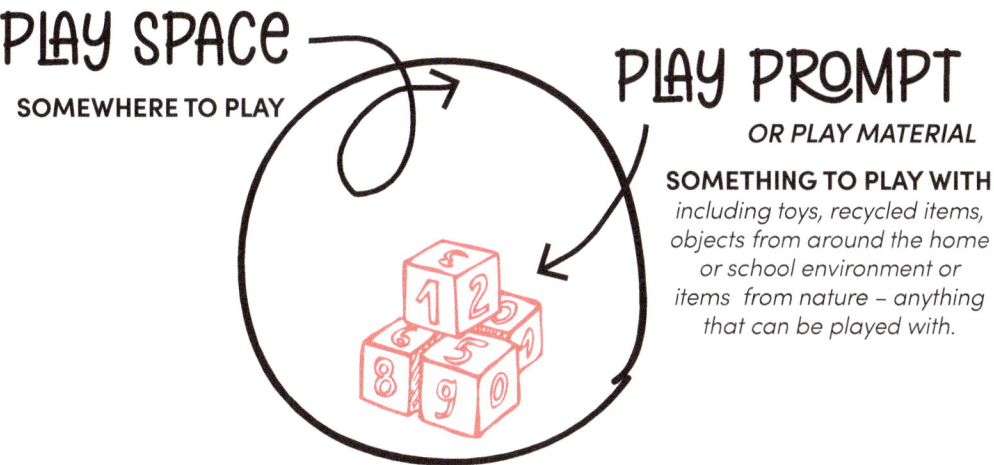

Play prompts in this age group include household items and toys that represent real life objects, either the same size or smaller, such as a doll, wooden car or truck.

Play prompts that represent part of their routine are important at this age, for example, for bath time, a baby with a little towel, for bedtime, a baby and a blanket, for feeding time, a bottle, etc. Depending on exposure, pretend play with a caregiver or older sibling can help some 18- to 24-month-old toddlers expand their simple play actions, such as feeding a doll to feeding and putting her to bed. In other words, acting out a sequence of a routine and combining more than one object as part of their pretend play. The start of simple 'vroom vrooms' can, with the support of a skilled playmate, whether in the form of a caregiver or an older sibling, set the foundation for many play adventures to come.

Two to four years old

In children between two and four years of age, we see a widening of their imaginary worlds and an ability to engage with and relate to others. They explore more movement patterns, may enjoy some light-hearted rough-and-tumble play and, yes, they enjoy making a mess. Toddlers continue to discover and learn more about their bodies, the way they can move and change their position in space, their senses and their physical strength. They may start challenging themselves in gross- and fine-motor play.

Between the ages of two to four, we see toddlers progressing from playing mostly with their close caregivers to enjoying the presence of others and playing next to other playmates. This develops further as they start playing with two or three other children. During this play stage, there is more engagement between playmates but not yet the organisation, group direction and interaction required to achieve a definite play goal. Group engagement offers opportunities to learn and practice turn taking and decision making in play. It also allows for further development of their problem solving skills.

Their pretend play includes sequences from routines, life experiences, outings or holidays with which they are familiar. Familiarity is important as this allows them access to language, associated movements and actions as they re-enact the event or role as part of a play script. Therefore, the emphasis of their play themes often continues to be on domestic play and routines, but it may also represent scenes or characters from storybooks, movies or television shows.

Play prompts that represent parts of their routine and domestic play, such as *home corners*, with a small table and chairs or kitchenettes with smaller versions of pots, pans, brooms and so on, are important during this play stage, as they need props to enter into the particular role or scenario.

From three years old, skilled players develop the ability to use one toy to represent another, for example a block turning into a phone, as their abstract and symbolic thinking develops. Furthermore, their ability to understand another's needs and feelings starts to deepen, as they assign feelings of anger or sadness to a doll, or another character, during play engagements.

Age mixing during this play stage can benefit both younger and older playmates. Younger playmates can expand their pretense and social skills through exposure to and playing with an older playmate. Older playmates learn how to explain the intricacies of a game, may need to work out ways to adapt games for younger players, co-regulate and care for a younger player who is sad or upset and can even have the opportunity to find a playmate at a similar skill level to practise skills with which they may be struggling.

Four to six years old

Children aged four to six years mostly prefer to play with other children, rather than playing alone, with leaders emerging during group play. Children in this age group become more goal directed and experience pride in their various creations. Their gross motor coordination continues to develop, often through various tests of strength they set for themselves, such as who can jump the furthest or the highest or who can run fastest. Their fine motor control and tool manipulation allow for more recognisable end products in this stage. From the initial experiences of Pictionary game night flashbacks of saying, 'Ah yes, that's a lovely man … oh yes, yes, sorry I meant house' when looking at a scribbled picture, to being able to spot a tree or rocket ship with confidence as the details and accuracy of their drawings develop.

During this play stage, there is more cooperation between playmates. They may enjoy playing in groups of two to three initially and then expand to groups of three to six playmates. Our four- and five-year olds are still learning the finesse of turn taking, being the leader and negotiating play ideas. Over time, and with modelling and practise with caregivers, our five- and six-year-olds become more skilled at turn taking, compromising to facilitate play, e.g. saying, 'You choose a game today and I will choose tomorrow,' and negotiating to ensure that all players' needs are met. They discover that for a game to continue, all players need to have fun and experience joy, as an unhappy player may cause the game to come to a screeching halt.

> **tip!**
> Rather than guessing what a child has drawn, comment on the lines, marks and colours used in the picture. For example, say, 'I can see that you used a lot of red here'. They will often follow up by remarking what it is or explaining more, for example, they may say, 'Yes, that's the big red car we are driving in!'

Similar to the previous age group, age mixing provides a wonderful opportunity for older play mentors to care for, assist and guide younger players through the play process. This allows them to model and practise perspective taking, empathy, problem solving and negotiation skills as they try to help younger players during disagreements to make the game fair and fun.

Pretend play is more organised during this play stage, with group direction and roles to achieve a particular play goal and script, e.g. a teacher and students, a chef, waiter and diners or astronauts and aliens.

Children in this age group enjoy dressing up and having costumes and various props as part of their play themes. Play themes now range from domestic play, story books, movies and television shows (similar to the previous play stage) to their own creations, made up stories and, at times, combining different play themes.

Children in the later stage of this age group (and highly skilled younger players) can be observed playing and pretending without the use of props, as their ability to re-enact and stay in character develops. They may also assign character roles to inanimate objects, such as their stuffed animals.

Children become more skilled at using open-ended toys and objects in their play engagements. As the child's flexible and creative thinking expands, one can observe their ability to change the properties of these open-ended items during play, such as a box turning into a rocket ship or a pizza oven.

Some children may struggle to use open-ended objects during play. You may hear remarks such as, 'That's silly, you can't talk on a block' or, 'No, that's not a rocket ship, it is just a box.' Throughout my years of playground observations and play assessments, there appears to have been a decline in some (but not all) children's ability to use open-ended play prompts and everyday objects in unconventional and creative ways during play. For some children, their pretend play may involve line-for-line scripted and copied dialogue from a movie or show, replicating the exact narrative, rather than using that as inspiration and adapting it as part of their own play adventure. Re-enacting the show or movie does not necessarily allow for the play engagement to evolve or adapt and may create disagreements between playmates.

When a child has difficulty in stepping into fantasy play, where the play is spontaneous and not necessarily reality bound (or based exactly on a television show or movie) and where the play may evolve at any time, this could result in them being excluded from group play opportunities. This may be observed in a child 'choosing' solitary play over group play, as the other children's games are deemed to be 'silly', or the child being excluded by their peers, as playmates feel they are unable to adapt to the play script and play role as part of the game, resulting in their part coming to a sudden, premature end.

Unfortunately, when a child repeatedly misses out on group play at this age, they miss opportunities to develop various socio-emotional skills, as well as executive functioning, problem solving, perspective taking and empathy skills, which can further impact on peer relations during later schooling.

With that being said, let's take a look at the social play stages in more depth.

SOCIAL PLAY STAGES

Mildred Parten Newhall (1932) identified and described six social play stages through which children progress. You may observe some of these play stages at varying ages and you may find that some of the suggested timeframes differ slightly with what you experience with your little one. I have included a few notes and considerations for caregivers under each of these play stages.

Unoccupied play stage

Babies may play differently to the mental picture that some adults have of play. Yes, we need to stimulate babies, but we must also be wary of overstimulation. Therefore, aim to balance the time spent actively stimulating babies with opportunities for them to engage in unoccupied play.

Unoccupied play is most often observed during the first 12 months. From the outside, it may appear that their body movements and gestures have no clear objective. However, all movements, from kicking in the air to reaching or manoeuvring, are attempts to discover and strengthen their bodies and to learn more about their surrounding sensory and physical environment. This play stage includes observation and exploration, as well as repetition of movements and actions, which is very important for their physical development.

Solitary play stage

Parten noted that this play stage is most often observed between the ages of one and three years and can be identified as children focussing on their own play activity and not seeming to notice other children nearby. Through my sensory integrative lens, I feel that it is important for children of varying ages to have an opportunity to engage in solitary play. As I mentioned earlier, under contextual factors that have contributed to the shifts in play trends, children's days are longer, and their schedules filled up more than in previous generations. Solitary play can give children an opportunity to regulate their nervous systems. It also has other benefits that I will mention below. As with adults, some *me time* can be important when overscheduling and long school days are often a part of their day-to-day experience. A balance of solitary and social play opportunities can be beneficial.

Many, but not all, children struggle with boredom. They struggle to transcend the boredom space into play. Yes, as we will discuss, environmental factors, including the physical layout of a play space, the number of toys or play prompts as well as the caregiver's cues, can support or inhibit their ability to move from, 'I'm bored' to a play adventure. Along with the shift in play trends, some children's ability to occupy themselves independently in play has decreased or disappeared altogether.

Solitary play gives children the opportunity to explore and create without any externally imposed right or wrong rules. They learn to problem solve and work independently without the help of another player, which can be quite an important life skill. It can provide them with an opportunity to practise various physical and mental skills in a safe space, without the need to necessarily meet a certain standard or expectation. Therefore, they can adapt and grade the level accordingly as they experience success through repetition. They can grow in confidence, which may result in them bringing these skills into group play and their home or classroom environment.

During this play stage children can experiment and discover new play interests, which can further lead to a deeper sustained focus and flow experience during play.

Onlooker play stage

Onlooker play is most often observed between two and three-and-a-half years old but can be observed at different ages. During onlooker play, children can be seen watching others engaging in play. They may at times ask questions or engage in conversation around the observed play engagement but do not necessarily display an effort to join in.

Through observation, children are able to engage in the play engagement, without the intimidation of being physically involved. Children who are shy or slow to warm up may use onlooker play for a few minutes, or even a few play exchanges, before they feel ready to enter the play game. They may be using the time to warm-up to the play exchange and to understand the context of the play game, the play script, the players, the varying roles and how they could potentially enter the play exchange.

This is different to a child who is always on the side-line, who never enters due to difficulties or specific play needs that they may have. It is important as a caregiver, whether a teacher or parent, to observe for extended periods of onlooker, solitary or parallel play in the older age groups.

> **Children with sensory processing disorder, autism spectrum disorder, motor planning difficulties (dyspraxia), ADHD physical limitations or impairments and/or developmental delays may be at risk of being on the side-lines of play engagements rather than actively participating. We will discuss this more under the Play for All section.**

Adults are sometimes quick to say, 'Go run over and play with those kids,' rather than supporting and encouraging them to enter the play exchange in a gentler manner. Take a minute and reflect on the different personalities we may come across at a dinner party, or even how your own engagements may differ between a one-on-one interaction and a group interaction. Some adults also need time to warm up to social interactions. Let's not forget to afford that same opportunity to children as well.

First, observe the child engaged in onlooker play. Get a sense of how long, how frequently and possibly, why this happens. Consider how or when you may be able to assist the child in building a bridge between themselves and the play engagement, instead of simply yelling, 'Go, run over and play.' This may be in the form of encouraging them to get closer through other means, such as sharing materials or play prompts with the other children, handing them an extra block to add to the height of the tower or passing the ball back to them when it is kicked too far. Consider whether your involvement is necessary to assist some children in building a bridge to get closer to the play engagement, while also being respectful that they may need some time to warm up before jumping into the play exchange.

Parallel play stage

Parallel play is most often observed between two and three-and-a-half years old, although age ranges may differ. This play stage is observed when children play in close proximity to one another. They may mimic each other's play actions, use similar toys or play prompts and may even share materials. However, they lack group involvement, and their main focus is on their own play activity or output, for example each building their own separate tower.

For most children, parallel play serves as a bridge to later social play stages. However, as I mentioned earlier, some children with particular play needs may get stuck in solitary, onlooker or parallel play and require support to assist in scaffolding play engagements and expanding their social play skills.

Associative play stage

This play stage is most common between three and four years old and promotes cooperation, socialisation with others and further development of language skills. Children may have a similar play goal in mind during a play exchange, but there is no formal group organisation, no self-chosen, designated leader and followers and no particular set of rules or exact play script that children abide by. This may be observed in a small group of children putting on a musical show, with two pretending to play air guitars and one banging away on boxes as drums. They may all be in the same 'show', but they are usually playing different songs. One band member may suddenly decide to go build blocks instead, while the others continue for a little longer. They have the same goal but far less formal organisation and preparation prior to and during the play exchange.

As caregivers, it is helpful to provide a variety of play materials, especially in a play school or preschool context, that allow for practicing the finesse of turn taking and sharing, a skill that will continue to develop in the next play stage.

Cooperative or collaborative play stage

This social play stage occurs between four and six years of age. This play stage is not often observed at younger ages due to the set of organisational and social skills required for play participation within a group.

Play during this social play stage is organised, with an overall group goal and a leader that organises the play roles, script and sequence of events. This stage promotes the development of various socio-emotional and communication skills as they share ideas, develop the finesse of sharing and turn taking and practice negotiation of roles, play scripts, play prompts and sequence of events.

In this play stage, children collaborate in choosing a particular play theme and script, preparing the scene, selecting suitable play prompts and describing and deciding roles and sequences of events prior to starting the play engagement.

Caregivers should be wary of solving all problems on the playground for children during this play stage but rather embrace the opportunity to support negotiation, introduce and practise problem solving, guide the children towards empathy and understanding through perspective taking, co-regulation and modelling.

Frame breaks

Have you noticed frame breaks in play?

The director or leader may include a frame break in which the play engagement is temporarily paused to remind a character of their line or action, to remind players that a sequence or event was skipped or to get the play back on track if, for example, the policeman went off on their own adventure. After the frame break, the play engagement is resumed. This is much like a pause-and-play effect.

PLAY CATEGORIES

There is not one set, defined version of the categories of play. I am going to use (and slightly adapt) the categories of play as outlined in Peter Gray's book, *Free to Learn*. The aim of this section is to make you aware of the various categories of play (although different authors may use different labels or categories), which will allow you to observe and reflect on whether your child's play may be restricted to one or a limited number of play categories and to give you an understanding of the importance of engagement across play categories and the power of play interests.

Physical (and sensory) play

This play category taps into gross motor coordination and movement skills and helps to develop strong and coordinated bodies. You would have noted that I have added sensory in brackets, as our inner senses, namely the proprioceptive and vestibular senses, play a critical role in providing our body with information and feedback regarding our *internal body map*, i.e. our body schema and awareness that forms the foundation of our gross motor, balance and coordination skills. Furthermore, our other sensory systems are involved during physical play and the other play categories listed in this section.

The physical play category includes chasing, climbing on jungle gyms and other apparatus, lifting and moving large, loose parts as part of an indoor or outdoor adventure, planning, building and creating obstacle courses and, yes, risky play.

> **The proprioceptive sensory system receives and processes information from our joints and the stretch receptors in our muscles. This system provides input regarding the position of our body and body parts in space, the location, direction and pace of our movements and the amount of force a muscle is exerting.**
>
> **The vestibular sensory system receives and processes information from structures and cells located in our inner ear. The vestibular system plays a role in head and body position, muscle tone, posture, balance and coordination.**

Risky play essentially refers to the thrill of play that also involves a chance of bumps and bruises, in other words, the possibility of a physical injury. It is seeking a type of play that borders on both fear and excitement. This range includes riding a bicycle as fast as you can, jumping off a couch and crashing onto a pillow mountain or climbing up a tree or jungle gym apparatus. Yes, these are all examples of risky play, with varying degrees and ranges of possible injury, but all of these form part of healthy risky play.

Risky play allows children to explore their body and their capabilities. It allows for cause and effect and problem solving as they adapt and make adjustments during play to jump further, climb higher or ride their bicycle faster than last time. Children will often adapt the challenge as their skills and capabilities improve. The very label of this group of play may cause caregivers' throats to close. Perhaps it could be renamed to adventure-seeking play or possible-bump-and-bruise play.

Risky play primarily takes place outdoors, as part of physical or gross motor play, and most often as part of children's free play. As with other play categories, not all children will display the same interest in risky play. Research has noted a gender difference, with boys displaying more risk in their play than girls. I do believe that gender differences are impacted by subtle (and in some instances less subtle or even blunt) societal messages about what girls and boys should be playing in certain environments.

I feel the need to add that the opportunities for children who want to participate in healthy risky play have decreased over time. With an increase in litigation, some public spaces and schools have made various changes in playground equipment and the play spaces, as well as school or break-time rules, to minimise legal risks. This has contributed to a further decline in the opportunity for and access to healthy risky play as society has, over time, become increasingly risk averse in play.

The six categories of risky play as described in Sandseter's (2007) research include:

1. Heights

Climbing up structures, jungle gym equipment, trees, gates, various household furniture, etc. is the most frequently observed movement or action as part of risky play. This is often followed by jumping down from the height, unless they realise that they may have overestimated their capability as fear sets in at the top, followed by a retreat down to earth or a lower, more manageable point to jump from.

2. Speed

Play at high speeds from riding a bicycle as fast as your legs can go (with the risk of either not being able to stop in time or losing control) to the feeling of your legs running down a hill and taking your upper body along for a ride as you try to keep up.

3. Tools

Using dangerous tools, such as a hammer, kitchen equipment or perhaps a glue gun as part of a creative masterpiece. This category is performed under the watchful eye and close physical presence of an adult, who will first demonstrate the proper use and safety considerations prior to participation.

4. Elements

Being situated close to dangerous elements, such as at the top of a steep hill or near deep water. Children display varying degrees of awareness regarding the associated risks with regards to dangerous elements.

5. Rough-and-tumble play

This is often referred to as roughhousing or play-fighting and certainly divides the crowds. Rough-and-tumble play includes both play-fighting movements, such as wrestling, colliding, pretend karate, light boxing or no-touch punches and other movements or behaviours, such as chasing and running or sneaking up on or jumping out at playmates as they pass by. In other words, a range of vigorous body movements involving physical contact accompanied with playful facial expressions. There is never an intent to hurt or deliberate hurting involved. This category of risky play is more often observed in boys and requires players to balance their playful contact and engagement so that it does not result in physical injury.

In addition, I would like to refer back to the playfulness element of *framing*, which refers to our ability to read and give play cues to playmates.

A child's ability to correctly interpret and respond to a peer's play cue during rough-and-tumble play is essential. Misunderstanding play cues may result in difficulty in balancing the playful contact and back-and-forth play actions as part of the play engagement (on the part of both playmates). Research has shown that children are mostly able to correctly interpret rough-and-tumble play behaviours compared to serious fighting, even across language barriers.

Through the lens of sensory integration, children present with varying sensory needs. Sensory seekers enjoy, and perhaps seek, rough-and-tumble play, while children with sensory sensitivities avoid such play. Children with sensory sensitivities often avoid the noisier and busier parts of playgrounds, when compared with sensory seekers. Caregivers need to be mindful that a sensory seeker and a child with sensitivities will experience rough-and-tumble play differently at a body level, regardless of framing of play cues, due to their varying neurological thresholds.

There are numerous benefits associated with rough-and-tumble play. For example, it can help children to regulate through heavy muscle work and deep pressure input, which organises their nervous system; it may help to release emotions and/or frustrations; it contributes to developing body awareness and practising motor skills; it can give children feedback on what may be too hard, e.g. hearing, 'Ah that was sore' and having an opportunity to adjust their actions as they learn to understand and respect others' boundaries; it develops self-control; it can offer a fun, bonding opportunity and it is a good form of physical exercise.

Through this type of vigorous movement input, there is a balance between regulation and overstimulation in rough-and-tumble play. As I mentioned earlier, children have varying sensory needs that will impact this line and the ability to find the balance. It is important for children (and adults) to look out for cues, which children will learn as their ability to read non-verbal cues develops and improves, and listening when someone says, 'Stop' or, 'That's enough, I don't want to any more.' This forms part of a child's consent when it comes to their bodies and should be respected.

6. Getting lost

This category of risky play involves instances where a child may explore and roam an unknown environment, with the chance or risk of not finding their way back, such as exploring in nature or even an aisle in a grocery store.

So why do I care about risky play and, why should you?

In her research, Sandseter (2009) refers to the immediate and deferred benefits of risky play. I would like to use these two terms here to separate the benefits associated with risky play.

First and foremost, risky play is enjoyable to children. When the thrill and excitement outweigh the fear, the exhilaration often leads to repetition. For children it comes down to, 'WOW that was fun.' They are not motivated by the immediate or deferred benefits of risky play, but rather the process and enjoyment of it. Children enjoy risky play because it feels good and it is fun.

Now, to convince the adults.

In terms of the immediate associated benefits, risky play allows children to explore their bodies and their capabilities. It allows them to explore cause and effect and problem solving, as they adapt and make adjustments during play to jump further, climb higher or ride their bicycle faster than last time. Children will adapt the challenge as their skills and capabilities improve. This is the interesting balance between thrill and fear. When fear takes over, they say, 'Oh, oh no, too high let me go a bit lower.' The fear feedback helps to guide them, but so often, adults interfere before children can experience this body feedback and make an adjustment.

Other immediate benefits in terms of physical and mental development include gross motor skills, motor planning, focus, spatial orientation and depth perception, stimulation of various sensory systems, including their inner senses (the proprioceptive and vestibular sensory systems), regulation and, of course, confidence as they triumph over a fear.

In terms of deferred skills, throughout a risky play engagement, children learn how to assess risks and how to calmly master risk situations without their emotions overriding their choices. This takes a high level of self-regulation. In other words, this adaptive function later allows children to deal with emergencies and hopefully to make sound and calculated judgement calls.

So, now that I have convinced you of the value of risky play, you are probably wondering how to go about shifting the 'Be careful!', to supporting more risky play. You will find more information on that in the *Playful Ways* chapter, as we continue on the play adventure.

"When the thrill and excitement outweigh the fear, the exhilaration often leads to repetition."

Language play

This category of play progresses from cooing and babbling to playing with rhymes, phrases, grammar and more. Whether alone or part of their script in a dramatic play, the play on words and sounds, reciting, practising and engaging with peers all form part of the child's ability to grow and further develop their language skills.

Exploratory play

This play category refers to the discovery, manipulation and exploration of objects that spark children's curiosity and interest. They learn about the various sensory properties of objects, what they can and can't do and how they work. Children investigate various cause and effect hypotheses and mini experiments as they engage with and test the objects.

Heuristic play, a term coined by child psychologist Elinor Goldshmeid in the 1980s, refers to the exploration of everyday objects by babies and toddlers. The concept of a treasure basket allows little ones to explore the various properties of objects (textures, sounds, weight and so on) from their surrounding environment, which are rotated from time to time. Careful consideration is given to the sensory properties of the materials before giving them to the child, with a preference for natural materials over plastic objects that have a very limited sensory experience. Heuristic play is not limited to using treasure baskets but also extends to outdoor nature play.

Furthermore, play schemas, which will be discussed later as part of the child factors, speaks to the repetition of specific movements or actions that caregivers may notice at particular times, as a child explores and learns. The play schemas are most often observed in toddlers, and once a caregiver becomes more attuned to the particular play schema that interests their child at a particular time, suitable play prompts can be provided for experimentation and exploratory play.

Constructive play

This play category refers to producing an outer representation of an inner mental picture. The media may range from nature play with sticks, rocks and leaves to wooden blocks and art supplies. The child taps into numerous skills in this play category, namely hand dexterity, flexible thinking, problem solving and reasoning, executive functioning skills, STEAM skills, grit and persistence as they learn to remain calm when the tower they built falls over and they have to try again... perhaps using a different method, a steadier hand or different materials. This play category may merge with pretense play and other categories discussed as part of your little one's play adventure.

Fantasy play

This is the ability to perceive and create pretend actions and worlds that know no bounds. The elements that form part of this play category include using objects as part of the play exchange and taking on a role, a script (including language, body language and gestures) and a play scenario.

Through fantasy or pretend play, children are able to take on another's perspective, learn to empathise, practise social situations and improve future exchanges by practising or having a rerun of a particular situation. This play category develops social and language skills, encourages creativity and out-of-the-box thinking, gives an opportunity to develop self-regulation and, research by Badrova and Leong (2007) found, it can encourage and lay a foundation for later academic skills, including early literacy and writing.

Social play

Play exchanges, in particular associative and cooperative play as described earlier, offer opportunities to develop and expand social skills, from initially learning how to take turns to more advanced negotiations during cooperative dramatic role play, such as learning to be assertive if they want a turn in the lead role, taking on another player's perspective and making compromises and agreements to ensure that all players are having fun. The social play category merges with, and occurs during, the other play categories that were previously described, and it is critical to the development of various socio-emotional skills. As mentioned earlier, a child who is always on the side-lines of group play participation will miss out on the important opportunity to develop and strengthen the skills required for peer relations as they grow.

In summary...

Children need the opportunity to engage in play across play categories to develop their sensory, gross motor, fine motor, visual perceptual, cognitive, language and socio-emotional skills. One play category will not necessarily tap into all of these areas of development and, as a result, avoiding a particular play category may lead to gaps in the child's development.

The power of play interests may help the child to navigate and may expose them to the various play categories. However, some children may have specific needs that limit their ability to engage in one or more of the aforementioned play categories. In these cases, therapeutic intervention may be required to strengthen the underlying developmental building blocks that are limiting their play participation, in addition to using the power of their play interests to expose and expand on their play repertoire. Play coaching of relevant caregivers will be an important additional consideration in some cases.

PAUSE TO PLAY

1. What value does play hold for you?

2. Think about an example of an activity (non-play) and one of your little one's favourite free play engagements.

3. What is the balance between activity and free play in your home or preschool/playschool? Is there opportunity for both? Do you place greater importance on one of these?

4. Which of the contextual factors listed on page 24 do you feel have contributed to your little one/s having less time and opportunity for free play?

5. Which social play stages do you observe your little one/s engaging in at present?

- [ ] UNOCCUPIED
- [ ] PARALLEL
- [ ] SOLITARY
- [ ] ASSOCIATIVE
- [ ] ONLOOKER
- [ ] COLLABORATIVE

6. Which play categories do you observe your little one/s engaging in at present?

- ☐ **PHYSICAL AND SENSORY** (further including risky, as well as messy play)
- ☐ **CONSTRUCTIVE**
- ☐ **SOCIAL**
- ☐ **LANGUAGE**
- ☐ **EXPLORATORY**
- ☐ **FANTASY**

7. Does your little one/s engage in a variety of the above categories or do they have strong preferences for one category or a few categories?

8. If you answered one or a few to question seven above, do you think this could be due to environmental reasons, e.g. no exposure or access to a particular play category, limited play prompts to support engagement in the play category, individual factors, e.g. sensory or developmental needs?

"Caregivers need to go from serving the 'I'm bored' culture, to nurturing the 'I'm bored' space."

CHAPTER TWO

THE PLAY CONTEXT

THE PLAY CONTEXT

This chapter will explore contextual factors that either support or inhibit playful engagement. These factors fall outside of the direct control of the child but can greatly impact their access to, opportunity for and experience of play. This chapter will allow you to reflect on and consider which of these factors may be relevant in your home or early years programme. The chapter entitled *Playful Ways* will offer practical strategies and advice.

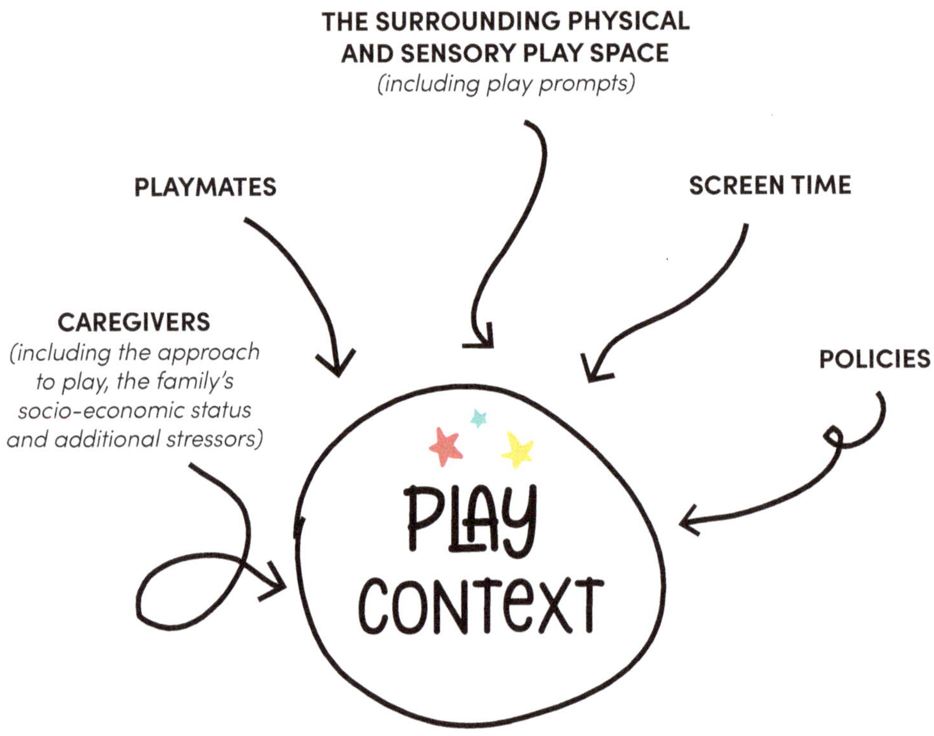

THE SURROUNDING PHYSICAL AND SENSORY PLAY SPACE
(including play prompts)

PLAYMATES

SCREEN TIME

CAREGIVERS
(including the approach to play, the family's socio-economic status and additional stressors)

POLICIES

PLAY CONTEXT

Figure 5: The Play Context

CAREGIVERS

The main caregiver/s will become a child's first playmate and play mentor. As a child grows, a caregiver may have multiple different roles or functions as part of their child's play (these will be further expanded on during the *Playful Ways* chapter), these include:

- Providing space, materials and time to play.
- Creating a safe and stimulating *yes space*.
- Observing for their play interests.
- Expanding on or inspiring play engagement.
- Assisting with play materials and/or requests during a play engagement.
- Being an on-looker or audience member.
- Participating and joining in their play from time to time.
- Supporting free play engagement.

In this section, we are going to focus on a caregiver's play style and beliefs of play and I will elaborate more on roles and functions later on as part of the *Playful Ways* chapter. The value given to free play by adults has decreased over time. Parental views have shifted, with many (but not all) parents leaning toward structured learning in the early years, in a race for their children to develop pre-academic and academic skills as soon as possible. This comes with a significant opportunity cost with regards to play and its associated benefits. Essentially, play has been moved aside to make more time and opportunity for structured learning at earlier and earlier ages.

Although many parents in the workshops and talks that I have done can reflect, with nostalgia, on their own childhood play memories, they seem to apply *a times have changed* attitude to play opportunities for their own children. They seem to have a sense that it is not within their control. There certainly are contextual factors that have contributed to the shift in play trends that we have seen up until now, but is it not within our control to make some changes, to choose between another structured activity for the day and free play or to reduce the number of extra murals and increase the amount of free play of a two-, three-, four-, five- or six-year-old child?

During level four of the lockdown in South Africa, we had an exercise window from 6–9 am. It was a joy to observe children running, playing and cycling outside in the suburbs. Some children have, for the first time, either learned to ride a bicycle or owned a bicycle, while others previously simply did not have the time or opportunity to go out and cycle. Yes, as the lockdown levels shifted and more cars returned to the roads, there were fewer sightings of families and children riding bicycles, but they have not yet disappeared altogether at this stage.

I hope we can remember the joy and laughter of young children (and adults) as they roamed free during those precious exercise window hours. I hope we can continue to bring play back to homes, schools and communities. I hope that we can find a sacred place and opportunity for play in a post-lockdown society, one that is not deemed less important than other activities or extra-murals, but rather that we can continue to make strides towards and advocate for the importance of play for children's development, health and wellbeing.

I want to add here that parents and families from low socio-economic contexts face additional play barriers that are impacted by larger political and economic factors, as poverty and daily concerns related to survival weigh heavily on their shoulders. Poverty restricts access to play opportunities, as economic hardships and unsafe play environments do not allow children from lower socio-economic areas the same access, options and milieu in which to play. The importance that a child feels safe, experiences a nurturing and caring connection with their caregiver and has access to shelter and food cannot be overlooked, as it pertains to play and play deprivation.

Caregivers have an impact on the time for, opportunity for and access to play opportunities more than they may realise. Caregivers' beliefs regarding play will impact on the play opportunities (and types of play) that may be available in a particular context. Some caregivers believe play requires very specific tools and toys and do not necessarily view playing with sticks or boxes as playing, but perhaps even nonsense. I again ask that caregivers pause and reflect on why they deem particular games or activities as play and others as nonsense. What picture do you hold of play in your mind, and what has contributed to this?

> Essentially, play has been moved aside to make more time and opportunity for structured learning at earlier and earlier ages.

I am going to take this a step further and introduce the idea of adult play styles. What are your preferred play styles and preferences that you have developed over time?

In addition to becoming more aware in guiding, rather than directing, play (which we will explore further in the *Playful Ways* chapter), it is beneficial to take a step back and consider the types of play that may be dominant in your home or classroom. It may be that, unknowingly, a caregiver has created a play space that supports certain types of play over others owing to their own play preferences or individual sensory needs.

As adults, over time we have developed our own play style that we bring into child–adult interactions. These may, at times, complement each other. Some adults may flourish in pretend adventures to far off places, while others struggle to swallow another cup of tea at the tea party.

The adult play personalities that I will include here are based on the work of Stuart Brown in his book, *Play. How it Shapes the Brain, Opens the Imagination and Invigorates the Soul*. I felt that it was important to include this topic, as I noted in some of my therapy interviews that one parent would mention that the other is *just better at playing with the kids*. Often, once we started engaging more around this issue, I realised that their view of what constitutes play and what doesn't, would come into the equation.

Therefore, some parents and caregivers may miss out on the play connections they share with their children, simply based on their own view and definition of play. I hope this concept of play styles will make you aware of your own play preferences and how this may at times support, and perhaps at other times inhibit, play.

You may identify with one or more of these play personalities. In addition, you may tap into a different personality (or play style, as I like to refer to it, because it can be dynamic and you may adapt your style within different environments or whilst engaging with different children).

PLAY STYLES

The Joker

From dinosaur noises to pranks, practical jokes, stunts and in-the-moment silliness, the joker aims to turn a frown upside down. What may seem like nonsense or foolishness, is joy found in the process of making others laugh. Our class clowns, all grown up, may very well find other avenues to entertain, as well as a younger audience that very much appreciate their comedic touch to life.

The Kinesthete

These are our movers and groovers. From a dance off during cooking to a fun game of chase, these are individuals who feel happiest when they are moving. It is important to note that competition in games or physical activities is not the main aim for these players. These players focus on the physicality and the element of movement that play affords.

The Explorer

Their exploration is not only limited to physical exploration, but also extends to creative, intellectual and emotional exploration. From music or poetry to a friendly debate on a topic, these players enjoy exploring different ways of thinking and being.

The Competitor

The name says it all, right? This is the person who takes the rules of 30 seconds very seriously or says, 'No, we can't just hit the ball around for fun, how will we know who wins?' They enjoy a competitive game, regardless of whether it is solo or in a group. It is not important who their competitors are, adults or children alike. If they can keep score or break their own record, they will definitely be keen to play.

The Director

These are the organisers. From planning a dinner party to events at schools or special clubs, they enjoy executing their vision. Caregivers who prefer this play style need to be mindful when it comes to allowing space for independent free play to unfold. This may involve less Pinterest and handing over more play to the child.

The Collector

This refers to both the collection of objects and experiences. The collector may enjoy solitary play experiences as they go along expanding their collection or connecting with other collectors who share their interest.

The Creator or Artist

The creator's joy is both in the process of making and the end result, from painting or gardening to fixing a car. The process of creating can be their profession, a serious hobby or simply special projects to enjoy on weekends.

The Storyteller

People in this category create imaginative worlds through novels, dance or acting, but also relive the experiences of the imaginary worlds created by others through watching movies or plays. These caregivers will not mind an invitation to a tea party and may very well be nominated for best supporting actor or actress in an action, comedy or drama role. This concept also extends to those who are charismatic storytellers on topics that they love and have a passion for.

What are the benefits of understanding your play style as a parent, therapist or caregiver?

Personally, it means being aware and, from time to time, being able to step out of my dominant or preferred play style and find the same rhythm as a child, which may mean stepping into a different play style altogether. There are times when adults can use their dominant play style effectively in certain situations, and there are times when you may need to step out of your dominant play style, especially when joining in a child's free play.

For caregivers, I hope this concept will normalise some of those feelings of, 'Ugh, not another cup of tea.' This is not going to get you out of the tea party altogether, but I hope this will allow you to reflect on what forms part of your play style and understand that some play interactions may come more naturally to you than others. My hope is that you realise that outside of the tea parties, you too are playing, perhaps differently and in a different play style, or play language, if you will.

You may be wondering, is it a bad thing to have different play styles in a family? In my mind, it is not. It adds to the very variety and flavour of life. I hope that you may reflect on why some play types, or categories, may be dominant in your home and acknowledge that your child's free play may have a different play style to what you are comfortable with, and that's okay.

Children are brought up in different cultural backgrounds with varying contexts, languages, social norms, play games and rituals that may inform their play repertoire and/or play choices. Culture can influence play. It is one thing to consider whether the play prompts in your home and/or school environment are diverse and another to consider whether the caregivers and greater play milieu support a range of play expressions or, in other words, diverse ways of playing. Do caregivers, or the play space, unknowingly (or knowingly) support certain ways of playing that may be influenced by their own culture. Is there diversity present in play? This will require a deeper level of observation and reflection by caregivers, especially within school settings.

I hope that this section has made you mindful of play styles, in addition to the play categories and preferences discussed earlier. It is important to understand what your own play style is and to be wary that it does not dominate in a particular context, leading to prescribing and directing certain types of play over others. In addition, acknowledge and be aware of additional factors that families and children bring to a play exchange, including their cultural background and socio-economic status, which may impact on their access to and experience of play within a range of settings.

As we will explore further in the *Playful Ways* chapter, a caregiver can have various roles and functions in a child's play. At times, they may want to show you a creation, share a triumphant moment or ask you to watch as they save their teddy from the other side of the river. Sometimes they may ask you to join in or to assist in part of the process. Overall, we don't want to become directors of their play but rather to assist, to help set the scene and to scaffold when necessary.

PLAYMATES

There lies magic in the transfer of knowledge and play skills from play experts that aren't adults, but rather playmates. In this section, we will touch on the role of playmates in group play and how they can support or inhibit play transactions. We will first look at age mixing in peer play and I will end with some thoughts on siblings and play.

Age mixing in play has benefits for both younger and older playmates, as outlined in Peter Gray's book, *Free to Learn*. I will summarise and mention some of the points here, as I feel it is important to examine the opportunity for children of varying ages to engage in play together. With children separated into grades, often with grade-specific designated play areas during break times, many extra-murals split into age groups and the decline of free play in community areas (outside of gated communities), owing to concerns around crime and safety, there aren't many opportunities for age mixing in free play outside of large family gatherings or aftercare facilities that cater for varying age ranges.

Opportunities for age mixing in play allows for play with playmates of varying ages with minimal adult interference, as older playmates are often given the responsibility to look after and keep an eye on younger playmates.

 There lies magic in the transfer of knowledge and play skills from play experts that aren't adults, but rather playmates.

The benefits of age mixing for the older child

The older child has an opportunity to practice leadership skills and learn how to teach. This occurs when the older playmates explain and teach games, concepts or rules to the younger playmates in a clear and concise manner. They need to break down, sequence and explain the components of the game, tapping into various cognitive and language skills. Older playmates will often be required to help in negotiating, problem solving and adapting the game, if required, to ensure that all players' needs are met and that everyone is having fun, for example, assessing and adjusting how hard the ball is thrown to children of different ages and skill levels to give them all a fair chance. They may need to step into a co-regulation role and help to regulate younger players' feelings through perspective taking and empathy. Furthermore, age mixing in play gives the older child the opportunity to find playmates at a similar ability level (possibly a younger playmate) to practice skills that they may be struggling with, in a safe and non-judgemental space.

The benefits of age mixing for the younger child

The younger child has the opportunity to observe and imitate during play. The Vygotsky concept of the zone of proximal development can occur when an older playmate can *upskill* the younger child by explaining, demonstrating, practising and grading the difficulty of play to ensure a just-right challenge. However, I also want to mention that this requires a certain set of skills on the part of the older playmate that is not achieved merely by a child reaching a certain age.

In peer play, there are varying degrees of playfulness (which we will further unpack in Chapter 3 *The Child at Play*). As part of this, children may naturally step into a leader or a follower role during play. A democratic, skilled and playful leader will attempt to make the game fun for everyone, take various perspectives into consideration and arrange turn taking for roles and ideas. The leader will not necessarily always be the main character but rather be skilled in providing gentle play cues, responding effectively to others' play cues and adapting the script or play game as required to maintain the fun. In other words, this is an example of a playmate who supports the play engagements of others and contributes positively to a play transaction.

However, we may have instances where one playmate will dominate or restrict other children's play, insisting on playing their specific game or in a specific manner, do not respond effectively to others' play cues or refuse to consider or incorporate others' play interests or preferences. Without going into the possible underlying causes of such behaviour, some of which may indicate a need for support, it is important to understand that, in this case, this playmate is inhibiting the play of others.

With these two examples, I hope to illustrate that, similar to a caregiver's role in play, playmates can either add to the fun or the frustration during play transactions in groups.

A highly playful and skilled older sibling, may involve their younger sibling/s in their play games, providing them with a role and perhaps bringing their play interests into the game as well. A balance of play interests come together and allow both children to bring their ideas and play scripts to life.

At other times, we may see an older sibling involving a younger sibling in play but with strict guidelines as to how to play, who they are, what they say and when they say it, with limited or no creative license given to the younger child to bring additional ideas or play themes to the table. Yes, in both instances the younger sibling's exposure to the older sibling's play scripts and involvement will likely stretch their imagination, and possibly a few other skills. However, as with the age mixing benefits mentioned earlier, sibling play can strengthen both siblings' skill sets in various ways.

We need to acknowledge that siblings may be in different social play stages and have varying play interests and play themes. Therefore, you may need to adjust that picture-perfect view of your little ones playing together for hours. There are various factors that will impact the ease and flow of sibling play, including their ages, play stages, temperaments, playfulness, developmental skills and even their moods on the day!

Sibling play, similar to playing with others, will allow for various socio-emotional and language skills to be expanded, when compared with playing alone. However, as we discussed at the start of the book, playing independently, without someone constantly providing ideas (perhaps most especially in the case of a younger child who is often following the lead of an older child, or a child who tends to always be a follower in group play within the school context), will allow them to work on coming up with their own ideas, developing problem solving skills, finding ways to occupy themselves in fun ways, discovering their own play interests, finding an opportunity to work on skills that they may feel a need to practice (in the safety of a play context) and learning to regulate themselves, to name just a few benefits again. Ideally, siblings should have an opportunity for both types of play and be able to allow that flow between playing alone and together. Balance is key, and this may look different from family unit to family unit.

A few short notes on sharing and turn taking. Like many other skills, these take practice. They require children to take on another's perspective, to put aside their own wants and needs for another's, to have patience, to delay gratification and to manage their own emotions. Once we unpack the word sharing, it reveals that there is quite a bit going on there!

Children will benefit from parents modelling desired behaviours, providing them with opportunities to practise, acknowledging positive progress and, importantly, being patient. Remember that, again, this is a skill that will take time and practise.

Focus on modelling, narrating and practising turn-taking during play and other daily activities. Say things like, 'I am using this right now. I will give it to you as soon as I am done. Here you go, your turn.' Engage in pretend play, which offers opportunities to experience and practise turn taking and waiting your turn. This could be anything from waiting for a cup of tea or waiting for your turn at the doctor's office to taking turns to be the superhero who saves the lion. Narrate the tricky moments, practise and problem solve together.

The following are some things you might say in these interactions:

- 'I can see he is still using the blocks that you also want to use. This is a problem. What do you think we can do?'
- 'I know you wish that you could play with it, but she is still busy playing. It is okay to feel sad, but we can't grab or steal the toy away right now.'
- 'Max, can you let Sally know when you are done with the toy?'
- 'Let's look around. What else can you play with while you wait?' or, 'What did you play before that was fun?'

Allowing each child five minutes to play with a special toy does not allow for deep play to occur and can cause a child to feel flustered, as they are rushed through the process. Become their co-pilot through the process of modelling, practising and problem solving turn taking. Sharing requires empathy and understanding another's perspective. This will take time to develop.

By school-going age, children are mostly able to share and take turns, as their self-regulation and socio-emotional skills continue to strengthen over time. However, during this period they have a strong sense of right and wrong, which may affect with whom and under which circumstances they are willing to share. Caregiver modelling and coaching will continue to be important.

The role and importance of playmates changes as a child goes through the various social play stages, from main caregivers initially being their playmates, to an expanding social world as the child grows. Free play with peers allows children to learn various socio-emotional skills, collaboration, negotiation, compromise, perspective taking and empathy, while also allowing them to experience social connection and, essentially, to become social beings.

"Children will benefit from parents modelling desired behaviours, providing them with opportunities to practise, acknowledging positive progress, and, importantly, being patient."

THE PHYSICAL AND SENSORY PLAY ENVIRONMENT

I believe that playful moments can happen anywhere, any time. However, through play observations done in varying contexts and school settings, it has become apparent that certain home or school environments will lend themselves more to certain types or categories of play than others. For example, the amount of physical or risky play that can happen in a house with a large back garden and trees will be different than in a smaller apartment.

Therefore, it is important to consider play space areas and sizes, as well as the play prompts that are freely available in the play space. Which play categories are supported by the physical play space in your home or early years programme? Which play categories are missing? As I mentioned earlier, it is important to consider engagement across different play categories to ensure that developmental gaps do not form due to a lack of play opportunities in certain play categories.

This may require some families, or early years settings, to become creative in using their space, choosing prompts and rotating toys to ensure children have play opportunities across the play categories. We will discuss considerations and strategies for play spaces and play prompts more in the *Playful Ways* chapter.

Furthermore, from a sensory perspective, we need to consider how various individuals may experience a particular play space by considering aspects of the environment, such as:

Lighting and Visual Stimuli

Aspects to consider may include: how bright are the lights, do they flicker, is there an option for natural lighting, how visually busy or distracting is the play space, is the room decorated in bright colours and is there a lot of movement in and out of the room or play space?

Noise

Aspects to consider may include: the noise intensity or levels, does the room amplify sound, is there opportunity for nature sounds, the type and intensity of background music?

This thought on noise levels is not meant to quiet down play all together, but to become mindful of how varying sensory profiles may experience the same play space. Outdoor play tends to be noisier. This may cause some children with sensory sensitivities to avoid noisier or busier parts of the playground. It may be important to consider the opportunities to engage in all play spaces, with varying degrees of noise, to ensure that some children do not avoid play spaces altogether during dedicated play times. Furthermore, some schools or homes may be located close to busy roads where various traffic noises may be a constant.

Smells

Yes, this may seem like a strange one to include! However, I have seen play spaces that are in surprising locations.

Aspects to consider: is the play space right next to toilet areas or located close to drains or garbage bins that are not cleaned until the end of the day (or sometimes the larger bins that only get removed once a week), is the play space located close to kitchen areas where particular smells may linger in the air while food is prepared?

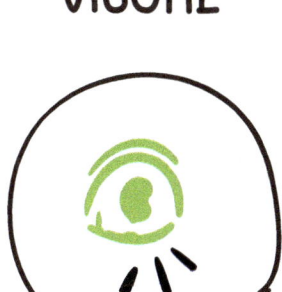

VISUAL

LIGHTING
COLOURS
MOVEMENT
VISUALLY BUSY
NATURAL LIGHT

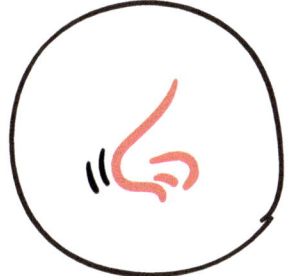

SMELLS

FOOD COOKING
BATHROOMS
AIR FRESHNERS
GARBAGE BINS
DIFFUSERS

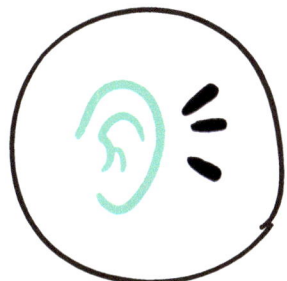

NOISES

NATURE SOUNDS
MUSIC
TRAFFIC NOISE
BACKGROUND
CONVERSATIONS

These are only a few examples to help you on your way as a detective. You may have a particular sensory profile that is not very sensitive to noise, lighting or smells. Children, particularly more sensitive children, will struggle to enter a deep and sustained focus in play if their sensory systems are bombarded with stimuli that they struggle to filter out. It may be useful to get adults to put on a detective hat and try to experience the play space from the child's vantage point by attempting to focus on different aspects of the environment, such as noise, visual stimuli, lighting or smells for example.

With regards to children who may have very specific tactile, movement or other sensory needs (that cannot solely be improved by altering the play space), they may require sensory integrative intervention by a trained occupational therapist to assist and support, with individualised recommendations regarding home or school adaptations. The examples above are general observations that cannot treat or resolve particular sensory defensiveness or sensory processing disorders without intervention.

SCREEN TIME

You may be thinking ... ah, not the S-word, Anandé! Yes, the pandemic has demonstrated the important contribution that technology can make, as most of our world moved online, but I do believe it also demonstrated to us the power and importance of in-person human connection.

For me, it comes down to the intentional use of technology. We are all on a learning curve in the digital age. Interestingly, each time I have done a talk on screen time I have had to update the information, as new research studies and information are being published, particularly on the effects of screen time on learning and development. This is partly because studies try to keep up with technological advancements and requirements to widen or adapt their definitions of screen time, as screen time use changes over time.

Technology can be a wonderful thing if we use it intentionally and not at the cost of other aspects of our lives. In practice, I have engaged with families using various approaches, from no-tech to low-tech to tech-rich homes where parents expose their children to coding from a young age.

The aim of this section is not necessarily to shift you from one category to another, but to allow you to reflect on your family's screen time habits, the quality of the particular applications or television shows, how intentional you are and whether screen time is negatively affecting other areas of family life or child development. When we are more intentional with screen usage, whether a low-tech or tech-rich home, care is taken to balance screen time with other healthy, active family activities and play opportunities.

I want to recap the screen time guidelines (even though we all know that these have been shaken up during the pandemic, with children's schooling moving online) by listing a combination of the most current recommendations (at the time of writing this section) by the American Academy of Pediatrics (AAP) and the World Health Organisation (WHO).

AGE	RECOMMENDATIONS
Birth to 18 months (AAP) Birth to 12 months (WHO)	No screen time, except for video calling.
12 months (WHO) and 18 months (AAP) to five years	Less than one hour a day.
Six years and above	Limits should be placed on the amount of daily screen time (two hours daily). The type and quality of media should be considered, and media usage should not replace other activities, such as play and sleep.

Screen time is seen as most problematic in our youngest children owing to rapid brain growth that happens in this period. Screens have a direct impact on the architecture of a child's brain and indirect effects on development, due to opportunity cost, namely time spent behind a screen versus time spent actively playing and exploring.

Screens cannot replace 3D real-life experiences that are critical for developing motor skills and a child's ability to integrate and learn from the world around them through their senses. There is simply no application, no matter how amazing the description sounds, that can provide a multi-sensory play experience like the real world.

Another aspect that I want to cover, before we get into more specifics around children and the impact of screen time, is the adult-screen relationship, which has also been called *technoference*. We can take the office with us wherever we go, and we are able to connect with anyone, anytime and anywhere. This can become problematic if we are more connected to the virtual world and disconnected from real life and those in the room with us. Children need opportunities to connect with caregivers, and we need to be mindful of the way screens can interfere with opportunities for meaningful, in-person connections.

> "Technology can be a wonderful thing if we use it intentionally and not at the cost of other aspects of our lives."

Unfortunately, if children constantly observe a caregiver with their head down in their phone, it can send a message that everybody and everything else is more important than them, which can lead to emotional and behavioural difficulties if this trend continues over time.

We need to be media models and not have double standards for screen time. This doesn't mean that you have the same screen time limit as your four-year-old. What I am referring to is that if, for example, in your media plan, mealtimes are screen free, you should model that and avoid the temptation to quickly check an email or send a message during mealtimes. If mealtimes are meant to be a screen-free experience, it should be screen free for everyone at the table. In other words, find moments that you can model screen etiquette.

Getting back to the specific age groups, as I mentioned in play development, the birth to two years age group relies heavily on facial expressions and social gaze, which is why screens can interfere greatly. Infants use a caregiver's gaze and eye contact to guide their social interactions. Therefore, we influence what infants pay attention to. If caregivers spend a lot of time on their phone, then baby is certainly going to become interested in what you are looking at.

Regulation develops through time and practise with a close caregiver. At each developmental stage, the ability to calm and soothe when we feel angry or sad, to work through frustration, tolerance and disappointment and to make transitions take practise. Studies have shown that children struggle more and more with self-regulation skills because the process of being fully dependent, as a young infant, on a caregiver to calm and soothe them, to co-regulation and practise with a caregiver, to eventually self-regulation becomes interrupted when they are placed behind a screen to soothe. Unfortunately, this wires them from a young age to deal with fussiness, boredom, frustration, anger or upset by plugging into screens and external sources, rather than developing the internal mechanisms for self-regulation.

With regards to play and screens, studies have found that if screen time is pervasive, children are less creative in their play, tend to mimic basic screen time themes, display less originality in their play, struggle to use objects in their play in creative or unconventional ways, have difficulty with sustained focus in their play (and class environments), can be more impulsive, have difficulty with social skills (including taking turns, eye contact, back-and-forth conversation and play cues) and struggle to identify their own and other people's emotions during play engagements.

Let's move on to media plans. The key word here is plan. It is important to be kind to yourself and to know that it is just that, a plan. It may not go 100% right all of the time. You may very well have different media plans for your children depending on their age and response to screen time. I think it is key to not use a keeping up with the Joneses approach. Rather reflect on your own family and work towards finding the balance that works for your family.

Once you have settled on a media plan, there needs to be consistency across the board with all caregivers involved in the child's care. It may be useful for some to make a mind shift between behavioural and outcome goals.

The outcome goal in this case is less screen time, but deciding on specific, more manageable behavioural goals can give a greater sense of control and may seem less overwhelming to some caregivers and children. For example, a behavioural goal may be, 'I am going to leave my phone outside the kitchen area so that I don't check my emails while having my family meal.'

This is specific and gives a sense of being within reach, rather than an overarching statement, such as, 'I am going to limit my screen time and check emails less frequently,' without a tangible plan of action. Decide on specific behavioural goals for yourself and your family members. Some families may first need to start with one small step, while others may list many and be able to make a big shift in a small amount of time. Find what works best for you and your family.

The following five considerations are important in media planning:

1. Screen-free zones

Decide which rooms in the house and out-and-about locations (perhaps a family dinner outing or going to the park) will be kept screen free. Ideally, children's bedrooms and rooms where meals occur should be kept screen free. Mealtimes serve as an important opportunity to connect and debrief.

2. Screen-free times

Screen-free times may link to screen-free zones to some degree. For example, if the kitchen or dining area is a screen-free zone then mealtimes will be screen free.

Furthermore, it's important to discuss the timing of screen time. We need to consider the way screens prime a child's brain and the impact this can have on class participation as they struggle to switch gears from the rapid, fast-paced images and sounds on the screen to the rhythm that forms part of their class engagement. Rather use the time in the car to connect, prepare for the day ahead, schedule and discuss what everyone is looking forward to. Exceptions may be made for long car rides (such as to holiday destinations), but as part of media planning, we are trying to consider the impact of screen time on daily routine and participation.

The weekday versus weekend question is also a popular one. Personally, I think this is also dependent on the family. If parents are working long hours during the week and weekends are the only time for that family to spend quality time together, it would be unfortunate to see all family members behind different screens. In this case, weekends should create opportunities for connection, not disconnection. Consider how the week is for your family.

3. Device curfews

This section refers to the time of night when devices are to be switched off. Some sources recommend that screens be switched off one to two hours before bedtime, and some studies recommend three hours before bedtime. The curfew recommendation is important, as blue light that is emitted from screens can delay the release of sleep-inducing melatonin, increase alertness, cause difficulties in falling and staying asleep and reset the body's internal clock.

The studies' differences in curfew times account for individual differences, where some individuals take longer to produce melatonin. Melatonin is important, not only to induce sleep, but quality of sleep as well.

Consider an earlier timing of the screen time slot. We want to calm the body and mind for sleep through play, bath time, reading and snuggling time.

4. Quality of media content

Not all applications, television shows and YouTube channels have been created with the same quality, intention and educational value. There is often little to no research to back up the quality and educational value that some base their marketing on. Be mindful of the wonderful descriptions that are added to applications, or falling into the trap of downloading free application after free application without regard to their quality. A strong focus seems to be placed on the quantity of screen time that children engage in, without the same regard for the quality of the media content that they are exposed to. *Common Sense Media* (www.commonsensemedia.org) has useful resources for caregivers and reviews of applications, movies and more.

"Pick any media exposure as carefully as you would pick a babysitter to leave alone with your baby."

- Catherine Steiner-Adair, 2013, p. 88

5. The extra 'screen-free time'

Before rushing off to sign up for an additional extra-mural or searching Pinterest to get extra worksheets for this extra time you have freed up, pause. We need to reflect and remember that for many children, their usual screen time is often time that they have freedom from an adult agenda and structured adult-led activities. If this time is filled with more adult-led activities, we may end up in a bad spiral with children who feel more stressed and anxious, rather than less. I am sure you know where I am heading with this... **let them play!**

Yes, initially there may be complaints like, 'I'm bored', 'I don't know what to play', 'I can't play' or, 'I can't play alone'. Some children may require more input and scaffolding to develop an ability to initiate and play by themselves, especially if screen time has been pervasive and the only means of entertaining themselves. It is important for caregivers to help them to develop the skills and confidence to become captains of their own play adventures. You will read this more than once in this book, caregivers need to go from serving the I'm bored culture to nurturing the I'm bored space. More on this in the *Playful Ways* chapter.

Before ending this section, I want to touch on screen time transition difficulties by discussing the effect of dopamine, or the *dopamine hit*, as some refer to it when it comes to screens. Screens, in particular devices or games that have a cause-and-effect relationship, in other words, something happens on the screen and I need to react then something else happens and I must react, contribute to the observation that children look *glued to the device*. Young children do not yet have the regulation skills to deal with the sudden drop in dopamine, especially if they were not well prepared for the screen time to come to an end. This sudden drop in dopamine contributes to the difficulty with transitioning off screens and the need for co-regulation, as they are still developing regulation skills (which may not be as well-developed if they are always popped behind a screen to self soothe).

Yes, timers may work for some older children, but for younger children who have not developed a sense of time, even sand timers may be hit and miss. Why? Well, they need to look up from the device occasionally to notice the sand timer emptying. Children who are glued to their screens often miss that the time is decreasing or that the sand is running out. Then, in their world, their caregiver suddenly shouts that screen time is up. They frantically look up and notice that the hourglass is indeed empty, and we have tears.

For younger children, there are a few other strategies that may be helpful:
The bridging technique, in addition to the sand timer, may be more useful in instances where you feel that your little one becomes glued to their device. The bridging technique is a way to draw them out of the screen and into the world. This is where you sit next to them and ask about what is happening on the screen. Who is that character, what they are doing and so on? They start interacting more with you and break the intense back and forth between them and the screen. This also allows you to see where they are in the game or level so that you can suggest a good moment to pause or stop for the day. In this way, they will have a few additional preparation steps, rather than a sudden shout of, 'Screen time is up!' from a separate room.

Prior to starting screen time, it is also important to discuss what will happen after screen time, for example, is it bath time or play time? Allow them to collect a transition item that relates to the next activity, e.g. a towel if it will be bath time or their Lego set if it's play time. A visual cue may be helpful to ease the transition from screen time into the next activity. For young children, preparation is key.

I would like to end this section with another quote from Catherine Steiner-Adair (2013, pp. 156–7):

"Our children are quick to learn how to use tech, but how to set limits and use it wisely requires more self-discipline and emotional maturity than most grade-school children (and many adults) have developed. They don't think about self-monitoring for time or inappropriate content, exposure to violence, or addictive potential the same way we do. If we listen closely to our children, however, we can hear how their media and screen activities affect them, even when they can't see it themselves."

POLICY AND CURRICULUMS

"Today families are caught in a paradox. We're parenting during a time when scientists increasingly tell us free play is vital to the health of our kids, yet schools and policies are pushing us in the opposite direction – in an agitated rush toward early academics. The gap between what we know about young children and what we do with young children is widening each year."

– Heather Shumaker, 2012, It's Okay Not to Share

Shortened school breaks, longer school hours, increased playground rules and regulations, school curriculums pushing early literacy, numeracy and writing skills to younger and younger grades, more worksheets, more assessments and more pressure all contribute to less play time and a view that play is less important than everything else.

The impact that policy and policy makers have on the lives of young children and the way children are expected to learn and develop cannot be overlooked. Although this contextual factor sits at a higher level, we can advocate for play, and we should have these types of conversations to bring the important role that play has in a child's life to the foreground.

I believe that the pandemic and e-learning have given us greater insight into how policy and curriculums may be failing a generation of children, with expectations of certain skills at developmentally inappropriate ages, endless worksheets and unrealistic lengths of sedentary and seated instruction that may be doing more harm than good. I realise that many teachers and educators feel trapped in a system that they do not agree with, but when does it stop?

In concluding this chapter on contextual factors, I hope you now have more insight into the various external factors that children cannot control but that can certainly impact their access to, opportunity for and experience of play. I hope you have realised the important role that caregivers play in supporting the magical play years, through an awareness of the external factors that may impede playful engagement and a recognition of the various ways in which they can support children's play.

There is a popular quote by Maria Montessori that says, 'Play is the work of the child', similar to Jean Piaget's quote, 'Play is the work of childhood.' I would like to shift this in light of how play trends have altered over time and suggest that play is first the work of the caregiver. What I mean by this is that we first require caregivers to support play, to trust in play and to treasure the beauty that lies in play, and only then can play truly belong to the child.

PAUSE TO PLAY

1. What picture of play do you hold in your mind, and what has contributed to this?

2. Which of the adult play styles do you identify with?

   - ☐ THE JOKER
   - ☐ THE KINESTHETE
   - ☐ THE EXPLORER
   - ☐ THE COMPETITOR
   - ☐ THE DIRECTOR
   - ☐ THE COLLECTOR
   - ☐ THE CREATOR/ARTIST
   - ☐ THE STORYTELLER

3. Do you feel that your adult play style may, at times, dominate or influence the play opportunities available within your home or early years programme?

4. Do you consider the impact of varying socio-economic statuses and cultural backgrounds as part of your early years programme (if you are an educator)? Are play prompts, such as dolls, representative and culturally diverse?

5. Does your little one/s have opportunity for age mixing in play? If not, what opportunities can you create? Is there a park or programme in your area where children of varying ages can play together?

6. How do you balance sibling play? Do you allow for time to play together and alone? Do you always expect siblings to play together?

7. Regarding the physical and sensory properties of play spaces, consider the following:

- Are there multiple play areas in your home or school?

- Does one area serve multiple purposes (for example a shared bedroom that is also the play area)?

- Does the play space allow for the following (mark all that you have observed)?

  - ☐ **PHYSICAL AND SENSORY** (further including risky, as well as messy play)
  - ☐ **CONSTRUCTIVE PLAY**
  - ☐ **LANGUAGE PLAY**
  - ☐ **EXPLORATORY PLAY**
  - ☐ **SOCIAL PLAY**
  - ☐ **FANTASY PLAY**
  - ☐ **SOLITARY PLAY**

- Have you considered the following sensory properties of the play space?

  - ☐ **LIGHTING**
  - ☐ **NOISE LEVELS**
  - ☐ **VISUAL DISTRACTIONS**
  - ☐ **SMELLS**

8. With regards to media planning, reflect on the behavioural goals that you can include within each of these categories.

SCREEN-FREE ZONES	SCREEN-FREE TIMES	DEVICE CURFEWS	QUALITY OF MEDIA CONTENT	THE EXTRA 'SCREEN-FREE TIME'

"It is a happy talent to know how to play."

- Ralph Waldo Emmerson

CHAPTER THREE

THE CHILD AT PLAY

THE CHILD AT PLAY

This chapter will explore the attributes that the child brings to the play transaction. In the discussion below, we will look at playfulness, developmental skills, sensory needs and play interests and how these may impact on the play transaction.

As I mentioned in the previous chapter, there are additional factors, such as safety and emotional needs, that can impact on play. The caregiver's role, in tuning into their child's needs and providing a connection and a safe and nurturing environment, is imperative.

In chapter 1, the different social play stages were discussed, demonstrating that children of various ages fall into different play stages. This should also be in the back of the caregiver's mind when observing their child in peer-play interactions, as they develop and progress through the social play stages.

In this chapter we will be taking a look at the following:

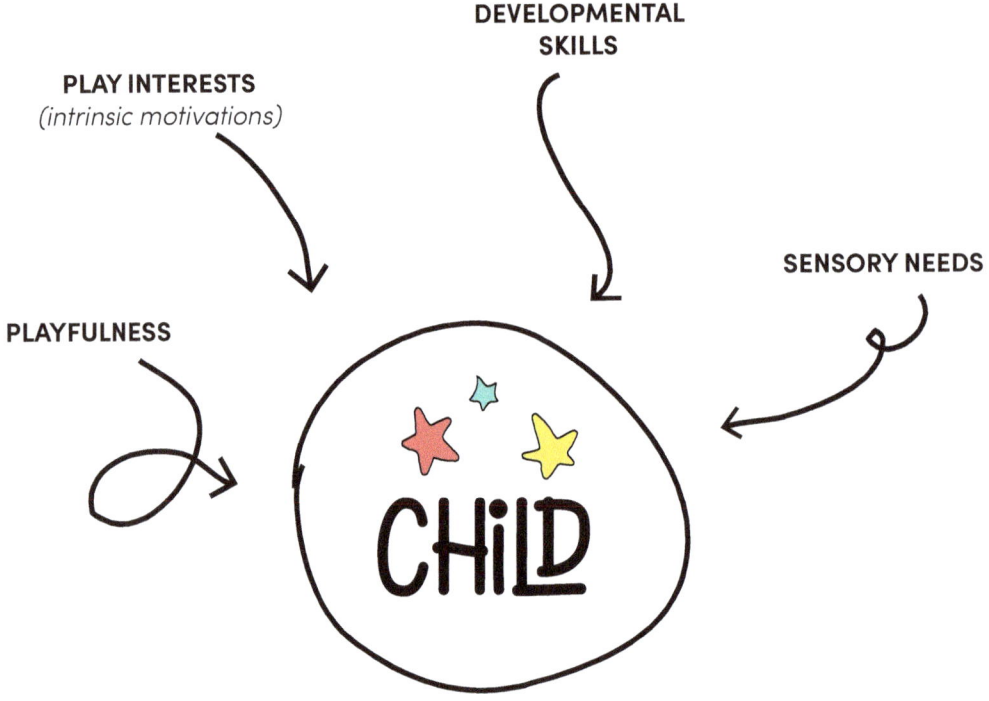

Figure 6: The child at play

PLAYFULNESS

Playfulness has been described as a disposition or drive to engage in play. We are all born with a level of or capacity for playfulness, which can remain stable over our lifespan. Studies have however, demonstrated that playfulness levels can increase when an intervention specifically focuses on this aspect. Due to neural plasticity of the brain, playfulness can be altered and improved through experience and repetition, as Hebb (1961) coined "neurons that fire together wire together". In other words, playfulness can be improved, similar to other developmental skills. Therefore, some children may have specific play needs, in particular playfulness, which may limit their play engagement. In chapter 5 *Play for All*, we will discuss the play needs of children with varying diagnoses, who may require additional support to further develop their playfulness.

Skard and Bundy (2008) described four elements that encompass playfulness: intrinsic motivation, internal control, ability to suspend reality and framing, which I discussed in chapter 1 as part of a deeper understanding of play versus non-play. You can revisit these definitions on pages 19 and 20.

"It is a happy talent to know how to play."

- Ralph Waldo Emmerson

A child who is internally motivated to engage in an active process of play without external cues or expecting a reward is deemed more playful than a child who engages in play for an extrinsic reward or does not choose the play activity, such as, 'Please play with this puzzle for ten minutes and then you can watch YouTube'.

Peter Gray made further reference to the positive impact of a playful and non-stressed state of mind on a child's drive to create and learn and the negative, stifling impact of rewards, assessments or evaluations. This reminds us again of the importance of child-led or guided play in learning approaches for young children, rather than being overly focussed on structured activities and worksheets.

Through improved playfulness a child's other developmental skills can strengthen as well. This occurs because as the child is driven to engage in play, they are exposed to and engage more regularly in various types and categories of play, tapping into and strengthening various areas of development.

Playfulness has been linked to higher levels of creativity, problem solving, divergent thinking, coping mechanisms, positive affect, regulation skills and wellbeing. Vital skills for the future, wouldn't you say?

PLAY INTERESTS

In this section, I want to expand your view of play interests being limited to particular play themes, such as dinosaurs, transport or movies, e.g. *Frozen*, and expand this to further include play actions that also form part of play interests, in particular for babies, toddlers and younger children.

Caregivers are often in tune with, and aware of, play themes that their child may be interested in. Play themes can be a motivational factor for a child across various play categories. If we take a dinosaur play theme, for example, they may pretend to be meat eaters versus plant eaters in fantasy social play, they can choose to build, draw and create their favourite dinosaur as part of creative or constructive play or they may set up a dinosaur terrain where they have to climb to the top of the mountain and then into a cave as part of physical play. Therefore, the same theme can be carried across social, fantasy, creative, constructive and physical play categories.

In each of these self-motivated play exchanges, a child will be presented with different learning opportunities and challenges and, therefore, a different set of skills to tap into. The power of a play interest can motivate a child to engage happily in a variety of play categories.

"The power of a play interest can motivate a child to engage happily in a variety of play categories."

For younger children, in particular babies and toddlers, who are learning about their senses and body, objects and the world around them will often do so through explorative play. Their play interests may look slightly different. Have you noticed your little one enjoying putting things together and pulling them apart? Do they enjoy pouring water or sand from one container or cup to the next? Do they enjoy knocking things over? Do they throw their cup or teddy over and over again?

A play schema, simply stated, is a repeated pattern of behaviour or action that a child engages in to learn more about themselves, their environment, the things in it and how these objects work. Piaget (1952) theorised that schemas allow children to progress through the stages of learning. Parts of his theories considered how schematic play enables the transitions between the stages. The theories on play schemas were further developed and made more popular through the work of Chris Athey, Cathy Nutbrown, Cath Arnold and Tina Bruce, to name a few.

Young children benefit from repetition, as these early experiences build and strengthen neural pathways, which make these connections faster and more automatic over time. We are born with neurons (specialised brain cells) that, with appropriate stimulation and supportive environmental factors, rapidly form synapses (connections or pathways) during the first 1000 days of life. These pathways become faster with repetition, while others that are rarely used become weaker and eventually, throughout childhood and adulthood, may be pruned away. The stronger the synapse or connection, the more quickly and efficiently information can move along the path. So, repetitive play during the early years is vital. Although you may tire when you hear, for the 20th time, 'Watch, watch this… ,' with the same outcome, repetition allows children to build pathways, construct meaning, master skills and become more confident explorers, able to take on a new challenge or skill.

I want to add here, as some may have questions around repetition in play and autism spectrum disorder, that there is a difference between repetition in play as part of a child's wider play repertoire and a child displaying restrictive limited play actions and/or movements while also experiencing difficulties with certain play categories. Children diagnosed with autism spectrum disorder may experience difficulties giving and responding to others' play and social cues, may have difficulty with joint attention and turn taking, find it difficult to expand play actions, may become overly focused on a part of a toy or one aspect of a game e.g. playing with the wheel of the car toy, rather than the whole car toy and may experience difficulty with imitation and pretend play skills. There are additional behaviours that one can keep an eye out for should you be concerned about restrictive play that form part of a formal diagnosis for autism spectrum disorder. If you are concerned about the amount of time your child engages in restrictive play along with other behaviours, I would advise that you contact your paediatrician or an educational psychologist for a formal assessment.

Your child may engage in one or more of these play schemas during a play engagement. Some play schemas often go together, such as building and crashing or connecting and disconnecting. Your child may engage in some, or all, of the play schemas at different points in time.

Let's have a look at some of the most common play schemas, which I will at times refer to as play actions, as I have found this description to be easier for caregivers to relate to. I have grouped some of the play schemas together for ease of discussion and have only described the most common play schemas. Observe your little one's free play closely. Their intrinsic play motivation may not fall exactly into one of these play schemas as, in line with the theory and the definition, there can be numerous others.
In the *Playful Ways* chapter, I will expand on these play schemas and will include ideas and play materials that caregivers can provide their little ones to support and expand their play interests. By providing play materials that are in line with a child's interests, you will see a deeper and more sustained play experience, more ease and, often, more frequency of free play as they immerse themselves in their play interest/s.

PLAY SCHEMA/ PLAY ACTION	PLAY OBSERVATIONS
CONNECTING AND DISCONNECTING	The child is captivated by joining, stacking, connecting or putting things together and, for some children, disconnecting and taking things apart!
	You may see your little one enjoying construction, train tracks, Lego, gluing things and so on. In contrast, they may enjoy pushing the built tower or castle over, pulling toys or items in the home environment apart to see what is inside, tearing paper or snipping paper into a million tiny pieces. In some of these instances, especially when disconnecting might be explored through snipping their own, the doll's or even a pet's hair, it is important to offer safe and appropriate alternative options to explore this play schema, while addressing the unwanted behaviours.
	In this play schema, they explore cause and effect and use fine motor skills and hand dexterity as they manipulate various objects.
ENCLOSING, CONTAINING AND ENVELOPING	Children may show an interest in enclosed spaces, covering or hiding items or themselves.
	You may observe children climbing and hiding in boxes, containers or forts, filling and emptying buckets with sand or water or filling boxes or a washing basket with toys.
	They are exploring the volume, capacity, space, measurement, mass, size, shape and spatial properties of objects and materials. Furthermore, enclosed spaces can have a calming and regulating effect on the nervous system, as external sensory stimuli are blocked out and a quieter, darker and enclosed, womb-like space is created.
TRAJECTORY, RADICAL AND ROTATION	The child displays a fascination with how their bodies and objects move.
	Does this sound familiar, the flying socks, spoons or even food? You may observe your child twirling and spinning items or themselves, watching the washing machine go round and round, pouring water from one container to the next, exploring running water, rolling items on the floor or turning knobs and buttons over and over again.
	They are exploring gravity and movement in different planes while also providing their bodies with vestibular input.

PLAY SCHEMA/ PLAY ACTION	PLAY OBSERVATIONS
BOUNDARIES	Children show an interest in crawling through a tunnel, under and through a table or chair or between furniture.

You may observe your child pushing items through holes, posting toys or items or driving a toy car or train underneath a built bridge.

They are exploring depth and the spatial properties of the 3D world. |
| **ORIENTATION OR PERSPECTIVE** | The child may enjoy looking at items from different vantage points, heights or angles.

You may observe your child looking at things upside down through their legs, climbing up and watching things from the top of a jungle gym, looking through holes or magnifying glasses or lying on the floor and watching things from ground level.

They are discovering how items or shapes may appear different, e.g. smaller or bigger, from different angles or heights, while they remain the same. Again, similar to the boundaries play schema, they are discovering depth perception and other spatial properties of the 3D world. From a sensory perspective, being upside down, or inverted, for short periods of time can further assist in regulation. |
| **POSITIONING OR ORDERING** | Children show an interest in categorising, sorting or order.

You may observe your child positioning or ordering toys or items by size or colour and lining up or arranging objects by a certain category or feature.

Through these activities, they are learning about order, categories, logic and symmetry. |

PLAY SCHEMA/ PLAY ACTION	PLAY OBSERVATIONS
TRANSFORMING	The child enjoys mixing different materials together to see what the outcome will be.
	This may be observed in actions such as putting food in their juice or drink during mealtime, mixing playdough, adding water to sand or mud or watching how food changes as it is cooked or ice as it melts.
	This play schema affords wonderful tactile, sensory play opportunities by including various materials that they can mix together. Children learn about cause and effect and what happens when certain materials, substances and/or textures are mixed together.
TRANSPORTING	Children show an interest in transporting themselves or different items from one place to another.
	You may observe your child filling their pockets with items, filling bags or pushing an item, friend or sibling in a stroller, box, washing basket or wheelbarrow.
	They learn about distance and how objects and other people move or travel between points. In addition, this play schema affords a wonderful opportunity for heavy muscle work through pushing, pulling and carrying items and others or moving themselves around.
OTHER EXAMPLES MAY INCLUDE: SOUND	The child enjoys shaking and banging different objects and items to discover different sounds.

I believe in the power of play interests and following a child's lead. It is important to be mindful of the adult agenda or competitive parenting, which may unknowingly influence the play prompts and play opportunities that you make available for your child. In *Playful Ways* we will discuss *loose parts* and the *invitation to play* concept further.

For now, I challenge you to first observe your child in play, understand and discover what their play interests are: from a play action, a play theme or perhaps a developmental skill they are challenging themselves to through their free play. NOT to discover what is trending on social media and to copy that exactly. Consider your child's age and play stage and then expand on their play interests through appropriate play materials.

DEVELOPMENTAL SKILLS

Children bring their own set of developmental skills, including physical, cognitive and socio-emotional, to the play transaction. Children can have varying play interests and not all children necessarily enjoy the same play categories. There is an important difference, however, between not having an interest and perhaps occasionally engaging in a particular play category and completely avoiding it because it is too challenging.

If a child were to completely avoid physical play, for example, they would not develop their larger muscle groups, coordination, balance and so on. The same is true for each category. A complete avoidance of a play category can impact on the development of the skills associated with it. In other words, this can have a compounding effect. When a child, who finds a particular skill challenging, avoids the play category associated with that particular developmental skill, they further limit their opportunity to improve at that skill. This can create gaps in their development, which can widen over time.

The power of play interests and using a combination of free play and guided play opportunities, can ensure that little ones engage in a variety of play categories. As I discussed in chapter 1, one of the cons of free play may be an avoidance of skills and therefore particular play categories that are challenging for them. The Vygotsky concept of the zone of proximal development through guided play can provide opportunities for little ones to further their skills through scaffolding by a caregiver or, at times, a playmate or group of playmates. Following a child's agency and play interests through guided play, can support the development of sensory processing and integration, gross and fine motor development, visual perception, cognitive and socio-and emotional skills which they can then further access and strengthen during free play.

SENSORY NEEDS

This section will not describe sensory processing and integration in detail but will provide you with some food for thought on the impact of individual sensory differences on play engagements and play choices. The purpose of adding this discussion on sensory needs is to make you aware of individual differences that may be present in your home or school environment. I have used Winnie Dunn's model and patterns of sensory processing (1997, 1999, 2014) as a framework for the discussions below to describe four varying player profiles.

Sensory modulation involves how we respond to and tolerate sensory input, how much input we need to register the sensory stimuli, to adapt to it and to have the appropriate sustained engagement and participation during day-to-day tasks. However, this depends on us meeting (and being able to manage) our individual sensory needs.

Sensory Systems

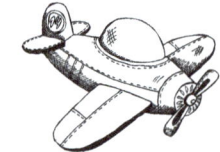

When I refer to sensory systems, these include touch, taste, vision, hearing, smell, movement (or vestibular), position (or proprioception) and interoception (the sense of what is happening inside your body, such as hunger, thirst and realising that you need the bathroom).

Individuals vary in how they process sensory information, with some having higher and others lower thresholds for sensory stimuli, and some may have mixed profiles. We can visualise these thresholds as different bucket sizes. The buckets illustrate how we hold and collect the various sensory input we receive from our body and the surrounding environment through our sensory systems throughout the day. We want to maintain a certain level in each bucket to remain regulated and engage in our various day-to-day tasks to the best of our ability.

Some individuals are more sensitive, have smaller buckets and can only manage smaller amounts of incoming sensory input. Others may seek out additional experiences and sensory input as they have larger buckets. Sometimes, there can be a mixed profile where you may have a range of small, medium and large buckets. For example, an individual could be sensitive to noise and incoming auditory input but may seek out additional movement input. This may be a little one who loves jungle gym apparatus and swings but dislikes loud screaming and noise from peers. Therefore, you can have varying bucket sizes and varying responses, either passive or active, to how you manage your bucket level (yes, it can get complicated).

Some children may seek out very specific play opportunities, to either manage their buckets, by emptying them a bit if they are getting too full, or by seeking out calmer sensory play experiences, while others may need to fill their bucket up, per their individual need, by seeking out more alerting sensory play experiences. Children may attempt to avoid certain play opportunities or play experiences at all costs (for example a tactile defensive child who steers away from sandpits and messy play) or may try and control the level and degree of their participation owing to their smaller bucket.

In this example, their sensory needs may interfere with their daily participation and the way they engage and learn in play, class, home and self-care activities. In cases where sensory needs, whether sensitivities or seeking tendencies, interfere with daily functioning to the degree that they cannot participate in chosen, desired or required home or school contexts, intervention may be required by an occupational therapist trained in sensory integration.

I have described the varying patterns of sensory processing, as described by Winnie Dunn's model, as different player profiles represented by four different characters. Through this, I hope to demonstrate how different profiles may respond to and engage in play exchanges. This has been influenced by my play observations and assessments of children with different sensory profiles in varying play environments over the years.

We are heading to the big top circus tent to discover more about these characters and their characteristics, and to learn strategies to keep in mind as caregivers. Come, join me backstage as we get to know them a bit better.

The conscientious ringleader

While walking up and down the big top, the ringleader looks around and exhales a big sigh of relief. 'Thank goodness I am here to make sure the show stays on track and that everyone knows where to be and what to do,' he thinks, 'I have eyes and ears everywhere.' Some circus performers have described the ringleader as perfectionistic, serious and even demanding at times ... however, keen detection skills have often come in handy, making sure that all the acts make it onto stage and give their very best.

'Oh no, the clown's shirt is back to front, how has he not noticed that? I better tell him.' 'Why, oh why, are they playing that song now, it's not time yet. Also, it's a bit too loud, we need to turn the volume down!' 'No acrobat, I can't talk to you right now, don't interrupt me. There is too much going on!' 'Please stop bumping me, you are going to ruin my clean jacket, and why are the clowns eating right now? The chewing is so loud I am sure the audience can hear!' he shouts as he covers his ears. Oh yes, the ringleader is a keen observer and will often make his or her thoughts known to others. If the ringleader is not able to manage the other acts, or the circus tent becomes too much, it can lead to upset, irritability and even tears at times.

Characteristics of the ringleader that you may notice during a play engagement include:

- Attention to detail in play.
- Enjoying predictability in their play.
- Noticing various external sensory inputs from the environment that may impact the flow of their play, such as noises, smells, touches or accidental bumps by others.
- Struggling to engage in multi-sensory, visually busy or distracting environments.
- Attempting to control play choices (including play materials, play script and play space) to limit exposure to unwanted sensory stimuli.
- Becoming upset when someone wants to take over or if they cannot be the leader in play.
- Having strong preferences for certain play categories due to sensitivities.
- Having a preference for smaller versus larger group play.
- Attempting to control playmates during a play engagement and becoming irritable if they can't.

A few considerations and strategies to support their play:
- When joining a ringleader's play engagement, consider the volume and pace of your speech, aim for softer and a slower rate of speech and use less animated gestures and body language.
- Identify textures they are comfortable with, movement input they enjoy and their sound preferences, such as silence or soft, steady-tempo background music.
- Consider how visually distracting the play space is. Can you arrange the area to be less visually overwhelming? Can you make it less bright? Can you block out or use blinds or shutters? Can you use natural light and neutral colours for play materials when possible?
- Provide fewer play materials, as they can easily become overwhelmed.
- When planning on toy rotation, ensure that they are aware when toys will be rotated, prepare them, keep their favourites out (they can be involved in this process) and make it a predictable part of the routine, as they thrive on predictability.
- Consider if there are any strong smells, such as kitchen, bathroom, cleaning products or strong perfume, and opt for softer and calmer scents or keep additional play materials and play space as unscented as possible.
- Consider if there are additional background noises, such as the television, that may interrupt flow of their play.
- Within a school environment, monitor how much they attempt to move away to minimise bumps and consider how to create a safe space for them to continue their play engagement.
- Consider if the play space includes a regulation space (see more on this in the *Playful Ways* chapter).
- They may avoid noisy and busy parts of playgrounds or play spaces, opting for sedentary play, so consider if they have an opportunity during the day for heavy muscle work or slow, rhythmic or other predictable movement input.
- Respect their time and need for solitary play.
- Consider how their play interests can be incorporated to expand play categories (all while considering multi-sensory play space implications).
- One more time, predictability in their play context is important to them as this helps to manage their smaller bucket size and minimises the occurrence of sensory overload.

The excitable trapeze artist

'Yes, I love the circus life!' the trapeze artist exclaims as they look out onto the arena, 'Bright lights, cheering audience, the smell of popcorn and hotdogs in the air, twirling, spinning, going all around. Oooh, have you seen my sparkly outfit?! It feels so nice, doesn't it? Here, feel what the sequins feel like.' The joy and excitement of the trapeze artist can be seen from afar. 'It's me, it's my turn to go on! Shhh... I have a few new tricks I am going to try today!' From the corner of my eye, I notice the shock on the ringleader's face when the trapeze artist leaps from one ring to the next... that may have been the new and unplanned trick.

The song has come to an end, but it seems that they are having some difficulty getting the next act up on stage as the trapeze artist continues to twirl and twirl high above the arena floor. The show's not over... after some convincing from other circus acts to keep the flow of the programme going, the trapeze artist does a final somersault and lands back on the arena floor. A soft mumble of, 'Oooh, my tummy, I might have done one too many flips', can be heard as they leave the arena floor. Peaking around the corner, I notice they have crawled under the magician's cape, a dark soothing hideaway after the excitement of the day.

Characteristics that you may notice during a play engagement include:

- They are inventive and come up with creative new ideas and play scripts, which they often love sharing with others.
- They seek input and are interested in exploring and engaging with various objects, play materials and, when applicable, other playmates around them.
- They may have difficulty seeing a play script or idea through, as they become excited about something new.
- They may not follow play scripts or the play directions of others very well, as they notice various stimuli in the environment.
- This may mean that group play continues while they start their own new game.
- Their play may appear disorganised.
- They enjoy multi-sensory play environments, play engagements across play categories and involvement of various sensory systems as part of the play engagement.
- They often enjoy being very animated in their play, including noises, big movements and moving props and objects around as part of their play.
- They are enthusiastic and often get other children involved in a game because of their energy.
- They may appear to be daredevils and take risks in play. At times, it may be necessary to engage in risk management strategies, see *Be Careful* alternatives later, and to give them clear boundaries.

A few considerations and strategies to support their play:

- When joining in a trapeze artists' play engagement, caregivers can be fully animated, lively and expressive.
- They enjoy multi-sensory play spaces and play opportunities, such as various textures, movement opportunities, being barefoot, background music, colourful materials and smelling objects or items as part of the play engagement.
- They will enjoy the challenge of new and novel play materials as part of toy rotation.
- You can engage in risk management strategies with them and find ways to support their healthy risky physical play.
- Although our trapeze artist has a larger bucket, they can become overstimulated as they reach the brim of their bucket. It is important to provide opportunities and time for them to reset and manage their bucket levels (see *Regulation Space Ideas* later in *Playful Ways*).

The endearing clumsy clown

'Oh dear, oh dear I didn't hear the announcer calling my name. Where are the others? Oh no, they are already on stage,' I overheard the clown saying while rushing past me backstage. While attempting to sneak onto the arena floor, the clown tripped over the speaker cord and bumped the magician, who was waiting to go on next, and their hat, filled with magic tricks, went flying. The magician doesn't look impressed, but the clown doesn't seem to notice and continues in the direction of the open curtain.

The ringleader is waiting close by and stops the clown for a closer inspection. 'What, my shirt is back to front and my tie is skew? I hadn't noticed ringleader. What's on my face, you ask. I can't remember. Mmm ... let's taste, ooh it's a bit of chocolate.' Awaiting the ringleader's okay to go on stage, a scarf flutters past and gets stuck on the clown's leg. The magician is close by, 'Here you go, magician. Are you okay?' offering the scarf back to the magician, 'What happened to your hat?' the clown asks inquisitively. Finally, the clown gets the okay and meets up with the others on the arena floor. While looking around at the audience, he doesn't notice that the others are now standing still on the arena floor, juggling. He accidentally walks into his one friend causing a domino effect of falling clowns and balls flying about the arena. 'I'm so sorry. It will be okay though, everyone. Let's take a bow and everyone will think it was part of the act,' he whispers as they all get back on their feet again.

Characteristics that you may notice during a play engagement include:

- They are flexible playmates and won't necessarily mind if games are adapted or altered. However, it is important that they are alert and stay on track.

- They may be slow to respond, or struggle to respond to fast-paced change within peer group games, which may contribute to a preference for sedentary, passive and/or slower-paced play engagements.
- Busier play spaces will not bother them, but they will need to be actively involved for playful participation, as they may become observers of others' play.
- They may appear disinterested in the play engagement, even when participating, as they are not necessarily as animated as others.
- They may accidentally bump another player without realising or knock over a construction creation that is being built, without any harmful intentions, as they do not process information effectively from the surrounding environment and their bodies.

The clown, similar to our trapeze artist, has a large bucket, but they will not actively seek out the sensory experiences needed for their optimal participation as the trapeze artist does. Some strategies will overlap between these profiles. However, in this case, the caregiver will need to provide more input and varied sensory experiences to ensure active participation. A few considerations and strategies to support their play:

- When joining in their play engagement, caregivers can be fully animated, lively and expressive.
- You can incorporate multi-sensory experiences as part of their play opportunities to alert them and assist in active play participation, e.g. various textures within the play space, from the play prompts themselves to playing on various textured surfaces, such as outside on the grass and inside on different floor textures; movement opportunities in various planes, such as side to side, up and down, forwards and backwards, upside down and rotary; background music, colourful and interesting materials; and different scents.
- They will enjoy novel play materials as part of toy rotation.
- You should include their play interest/s to encourage active participation.
- Consider safety within the play space environment, such as cords, sharp corners, breakables and so on, as they do not always process and notice these. It is best to adjust the *yes space* and to make them aware of these safety considerations.

The elusive magician

Peeking out from behind the curtains, the elusive magician's heart is racing. 'Look at all those people. Listen to all that noise. Ewww, what is that smell? Do I really have to go on?' The magician turns to the ringleader, 'You said I would be first today, and now I am number seven in line. I am not happy about that. That was not the plan. I like going first, before all the people are seated and before the smells linger in the air. It's too bright. It's too noisy.' The magician starts to ponder, 'I know, I will put some earplugs in. No one can see that ... my hat will cover them. Will it be strange if I go in my sunglasses?' The ringleader is not impressed with the last request, but the magician sneaks in their ear plugs and quickly covers them up with the hat.

Characteristics that you may notice during a play engagement include:
- They may avoid play opportunities or spaces that expose them to particular sensory input.
- They struggle to participate in busy, multi-sensory play environments and can become startled and upset by sudden loud noises or accidental bumps by others.
- They may often scan for or be on the lookout for potential threats, such as particular sensory stimuli or experiences that they find distressing.
- They may attempt to protect themselves by careful placement on the playground or within a play space away from possible threats, and they can become upset when asked to move.
- They may suddenly leave a play engagement if they feel overwhelmed or if the game suddenly changes and becomes unpredictable.
- They often prefer one-on-one or small group play over larger groups.
- They may prefer quieter or more sedentary play opportunities.
- They enjoy play opportunities that are predictable.
- They enjoy becoming familiar with play materials and/or play scripts and may become distressed if these are not available. In other words, they often have firm favourites.

The magician, similar to our ringleader, has a small bucket. Their buckets can fill to the brim quickly, leading to overflow and sensory overload. The magician profile will respond actively to their full buckets by avoiding, trying to flee or even fighting at times, all in a response to get to their perceived safe spot. Many of the strategies below show an overlap between the ringleader and magician profiles, as the aim is to manage their smaller bucket level.

A few considerations and strategies to support their play:

- When joining a magician's play engagement, consider the volume and pace of your speech, aim for softer and a slower rate of speech and use less animated gestures and body language.
- Identify textures they are comfortable with, movement input they enjoy and their sound preferences, such as silence, white noise or soft, steady-tempo background music.
- Consider how visually distracting the play space is. Can you arrange the area to be less visually overwhelming? Can you make it less bright? Can you block out or use blinds or shutters? Can you use natural light and neutral colours for play materials when possible?
- Provide fewer play materials.
- When planning on toy rotation, ensure that they are aware when toys will be rotated, prepare them, keep their favourites out (they can be involved in this process) and make it a predictable part of the routine as they thrive on predictability.
- Introduce new play materials to them when they are in a calm and regulated state and allow them to explore and/or manipulate the play materials independently.
- Consider if there are any strong smells, such as kitchen, bathroom, cleaning products or strong perfume, and opt for softer and calmer scents or keep additional play materials and play space as unscented as possible.
- Consider if there are additional background noises, such as the television, that may interrupt flow of their play.
- Within a school environment, think about how to create a safe space for them to play, or allow them to move when they become overwhelmed so that they can continue their play engagement.
- Consider if the play space includes a regulation space (see more on this in the *Playful Ways* chapter).
- Respect their time and need for solitary play.
- They may avoid noisy and busy parts of playgrounds or play spaces, opting for sedentary play, so consider if they have an opportunity during the day for heavy muscle work or slow, rhythmic or other predictable movement input that can help to regulate them.
- Consider how their play interests can be incorporated to expand play categories (all while considering multi-sensory play space implications).
- One more time, predictability in play is important to them as this helps to manage their smaller bucket size and minimises the occurrence of sensory overload.

The main purpose of this discussion is to make you mindful of the manner in which different individuals may respond to the same sensory input or environment. Play environments are a multi-sensory experience and children may therefore have varying responses to sensory stimuli that either support or inhibit their play engagement. Your little one may not fit exactly into one character description, or you may identify characteristics across two or more of the profiles, as some children can present with mixed sensory profiles and bucket sizes.

If we were to take this onto the playground, we may see our endearing clumsy clown playing happily in the sandpit. Let's call him Ben. The joyous giggles, songs and general happiness of playtime is in the air. A friend runs over and invites Ben to join their 'pizza party dinner', however as Ben stands up, he accidently bumps a friend who becomes very upset. Ben is terribly sorry and along with a teacher, makes sure his friend is okay before attending the dinner party which is located in the middle of the playground. He has a little stumble as he attempts to make his way between the children on scooters. 'It's very loud at this party' he comments as the host starts handing out pizza. 'No, I think we need music', the host comments, 'let's sing *Dance Monkey* guys!'. The dinner group starts singing away (all slightly different tunes and versions of the song). Ben is becoming distressed at the amount of sound around him. The singing, the pretend chewing and swallowing sounds, the scooters, the kids swinging close by, the cheering from the game of tag. 'I'm not hungry anymore' he shouts and runs away. Our endearing clumsy clown has disappeared, showing us his elusive magician side, running inside to the quieter classroom, to perceived safety.

Ben may have larger buckets and mostly appear to be an endearing clumsy clown. However, he has a small auditory bucket that holds a smaller amount of input and can therefore easily overflow and become overwhelmed in noisy environments and disappear like our elusive magician. Children with mixed profiles may respond differently within various multi-sensory play spaces, from indoor to outdoor play or home and school play spaces.

As I discussed in chapter 2, caregivers may need to put on their detective hat and try to experience the play space from a different perspective. Tune into the different noise levels, smells, visual distractions or the textures of pebbles or grass that may lead to a particular jungle gym. How would varying player profiles experience the same play space? Furthermore, do your own sensory needs, for example being tactile sensitive, impact or limit the particular play experiences within your own home or school context, such as limiting messy play opportunities? It is helpful to reflect on whether your own sensory needs may also be impacting on the availability of or access to certain play opportunities or categories.

In the upcoming chapter, we will discuss caregiver strategies and considerations for the play space and play prompts, including the concept of the *invitation to play*, *loose parts* and *toy rotation*. Do you set up an invitation to play that allows them to further explore their play interests or do you tell them what to do, how to do it and for how long? The intention behind these play strategies matter. Are you fostering play or setting up an activity?

PAUSE TO PLAY

1. What are some of the play themes, e.g. dinosaurs, trains or princesses, that you often observe during your child/children's free play?

2. Which of the following play schemas or play actions have you observed during your child's free play?

- ☐ CONNECTING
- ☐ DISCONNECTING
- ☐ CONTAINING
- ☐ ENVELOPING
- ☐ ENCLOSING
- ☐ TRAJECTORY
- ☐ RADIAL
- ☐ ROTARY
- ☐ BOUNDARIES
- ☐ ORIENTATION
- ☐ ORDERING
- ☐ TRANSFORMING
- ☐ TRANSPORTING
- ☐ ADDITIONAL EG. SOUND

3. Does your child avoid any of the following play categories (add anything you have specifically noted in that category)?

- [ ] **PHYSICAL AND SENSORY** (further including risky, as well as messy play)
- [ ] **CONSTRUCTIVE PLAY**
- [ ] **LANGUAGE PLAY**
- [ ] **EXPLORATORY PLAY**
- [ ] **SOCIAL PLAY**
- [ ] **FANTASY PLAY**
- [ ] **SOLITARY PLAY**

4. Have you noticed particular skills that are challenging for your child? If so, what have you noticed? Which play categories could this impact?

5. Which of the following character/s shared similarities with your child?

- [ ] **THE CONSCIENTIOUS RINGLEADER**
- [ ] **THE EXCITABLE TRAPEZE ARTIST**
- [ ] **THE ENDEARING CLUMSY CLOWN**
- [ ] **THE ELUSIVE MAGICIAN**

6. Does your child display sensory sensitivities that you are aware of or concerned about?

7. Does your child display sensory-seeking behaviours that you are aware of or concerned about?

8. Have you noticed that their sensory needs impact their functioning in play at home, school or in self-care?

If you answered yes to the above question, consider contacting an OT who is trained in sensory integration. The following link if for caregivers based in South Africa.

www.instsi.co.za/find-a-certified-ayres-sensory-integration-therapist/

For caregivers based in other countries, contact the occupational therapy body in your country for further information.

9. If you have children with varying sensory needs in your early years programme, consider the following questions:
- How can you rotate play prompts in the play space to accommodate different sensory needs?
- Do you have different play prompts and play space options for children with varying sensory needs?
- Does the play space offer a balance between the different play categories that gives children with differing sensory needs choices in free play to regulate their sensory systems accordingly?

"I hope that we, as a society, are able to reflect on the role of adults in nurturing and supporting play, not dictating it."

CHAPTER FOUR

PLAYFUL WAYS

PLAYFUL WAYS

This chapter aims to give caregivers tips and strategies to support and expand their little ones' play. You will not be getting lists of activities in this chapter but rather, principles and strategies. Pinterest and social media are filled with endless ideas for activities. The aim of this book, in particular, is to steer away from continuous structured activities and worksheets towards more playful engagement.

In chapters 2 and 3, we discussed various contextual and child factors that may impact on play. Keep the contextual and child factors that stood out to you in the back of your mind throughout this chapter, so that you can identify the strategies that will be most relevant to your child and family unit. We want to support children to become captains of their own play adventures.

THE ROLE OF THE CAREGIVER IN PLAY

I hope this section will empower you to move from serving the I'm bored culture to nurturing the I'm bored space, to move away from overscheduling, to move away from a push towards early pre-academic and academic skills that are not developmentally appropriate and to learn to trust in play. Studies have found that the push for, and insistence on, *earlier is better*, is not better. It does not put children ahead of their peers and can negatively impact on a child's interest and joy found in lifelong learning. Unless a child has a natural curiosity and inquisitiveness towards a particular skill, such as writing or reading, a forced approach will not put them *ahead of the game* in the long run.

First and foremost, caregivers need to value the importance of play. Once caregivers appreciate the importance of play to children's health, development and wellbeing, we can move towards more playful engagement.

When it comes to play, the caregiver role is mainly that of an assistant, not a director. Depending on your child's skill level, you may provide input in setting the scene, helping them access play materials, making time for free play in their day or routine and creating a *yes space* for free play. To observe for their play interests, to expand and inspire their play through developmentally appropriate play materials. At times, you may be asked to observe while they show you a creation or demonstrate a bold, new move or skill that they have succeeded in. At other times, they may ask you to join in or to assist in part of the play process.

It is important to be mindful to avoid creating a dependency, serving the I'm bored culture, by directing every aspect of free play or entertaining them with endless structured activities. Instead, support and create opportunity for play within your home by considering their play interests, play stage, skill level and sensory needs.

Adult-approved play or the *right way to play* can, at times, stand in the way of children exploring, manipulating and incorporating objects and toys during free play in unconventional and creative ways. Adults need to be mindful of the language they use in these moments. Things like, 'No, let's find you some round coins', 'No, that's not medicine, those are Lego blocks, put that back' or, 'No give me that and find something else to use,' can cause interruptions to the flow of play and may, at times, end the game. If you have selected play materials that you feel are safe and ready for your little one to engage with and placed them in their *yes space*, which we will unpack more later, support the flow of their play. Saying no too many times will affect the flow of their play and their ability to engage in free play with confidence, as they constantly receive messages that imply that they are playing *wrong*.

I want to add here that it may be beneficial for some caregivers to separate free play and guided play opportunities in their own mind. The caregiver role and approach will be different in free play when compared with guided play. If you have set up an *invitation to play* with the aim of free play, then it should be just that. Allow the child to combine and use the play prompts to their own heart's desire and keep interference to a minimum.

As I have previously mentioned, and will say here again, the importance of a child, first and foremost, feeling safe, experiencing a nurturing and caring connection with a caregiver and having access to safe shelter and food cannot be overlooked as it pertains to play. Although not represented in the three figures that follow, these are necessary prerequisites for a child to be able to fully immerse themselves in their play.

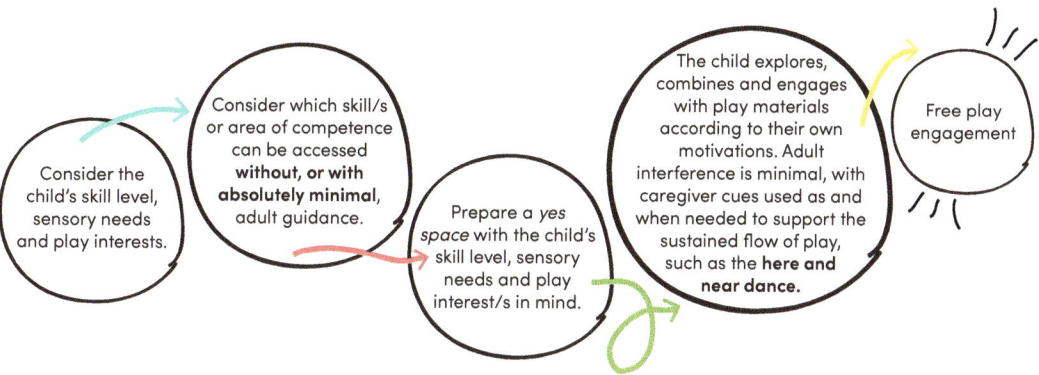

Figure 7 Free Play Engagement Flow

If you have created a setup with the aim of guiding play, scaffolding or exposing your child to a new skill or improving a particular skill, then you will use open-ended questions and inquiry. There is a dance between the child's agency and the caregiver's ability to know when to step in, how to facilitate, how much to facilitate and when to step out and hand back to the child.

This book, and this chapter in particular, will focus more on supporting free play, although I have mentioned, and will continue to mention, guided play, as I feel it is important for caregivers to understand the distinction between the two and the value of both. In a sense, these two figures (representing free play and guided play) aim to demonstrate the differences in setting up an *invitation to play* for free play and *invitation to play/discover* as part of guided play.

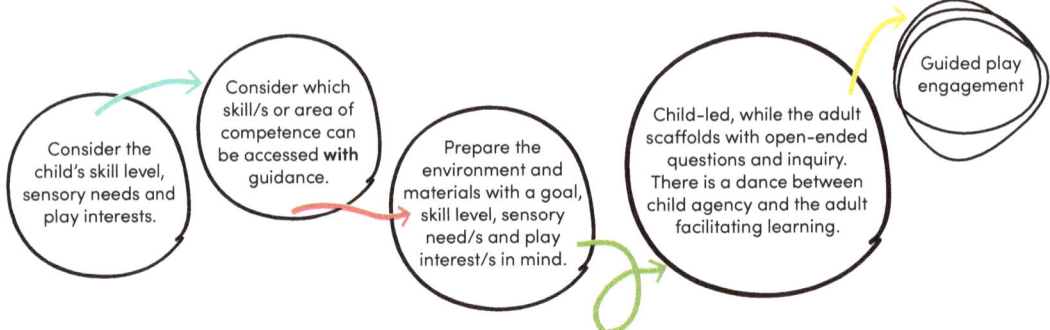

Figure 8 Guided Play Engagement Flow

Joining in play allows for connection and bonding and, furthermore, offers the opportunity to model socio-emotional skills, such as turn-taking and frustration tolerance. Through this process, play can offer a safe space to work through emotions, such as frustration and/or anger building up when our castle tower keeps falling over and can offer caregivers the opportunity to model, verbalise and problem solve with their little one as they build on their regulation skills. Joining in free play should continue to be child-led, and adults need to be mindful of not simply stepping in and taking over or completely changing the play script.

Do not play for your child, play with them. Create balance in the time and opportunities available for independent free play and joining in their play. In other words, again be wary of creating dependence on your participation and presence during their free play engagement and find a balance that works for your family. You will find more tips on this later in this chapter.

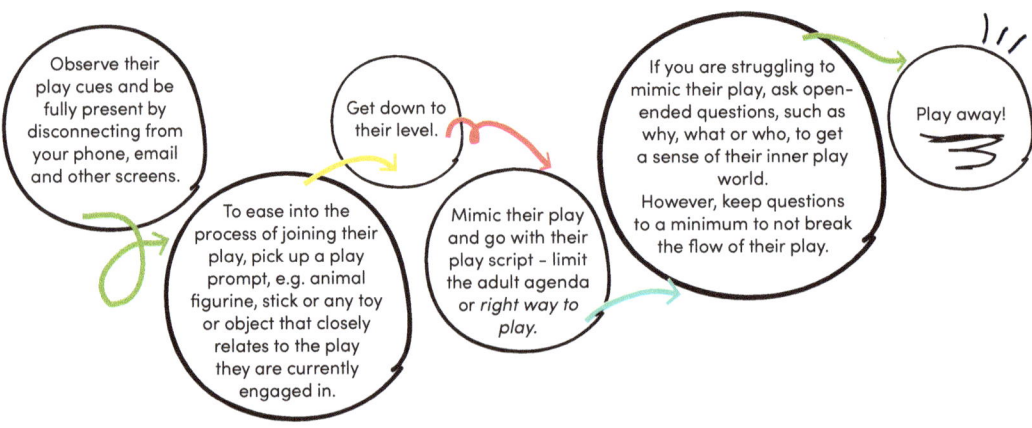

Figure 9 Joining in Your Child's Free Play Flow

Consider opportunities for connection throughout the day, such as self-care activities, mealtimes, bath times, pre-bedtime routine or special one-on-one bonding activities or outings. Consider whether your routine allows for daily one-on-one bonding and connection time with each of your children. Children who feel secure will be more likely to engage independently in free play. Some children may require time for connection prior to playing by themselves.

In addition, I want to mention here that, at times, neediness in play, i.e. a child wanting you to play with them or requesting that you watch them or be very close, can be their way of talking through the medium of play and processing difficult life circumstances or big changes in their lives, such as relocating, difficulties at school, divorce, underlying emotional difficulties or anxiety. These instances require connection and the opportunity to process big emotions with you, not alone.

If you and your family have gone through a big change or a difficult event, or your little one is experiencing difficulties and you have noticed more instances of your child requesting opportunities to play, reflect on whether they are asking for more opportunities for connection before you use one of the caregiver cues later in this chapter. Furthermore, consider reaching out to a psychologist and/or trained play therapist if you have concerns about your child's emotional wellbeing, or if your family has experienced difficulty in your home context.

DEVELOPMENTAL CONSIDERATIONS AND PLAY STAGES

It can be easy to get lost in the hashtags and posts on social media. Unfortunately, as wonderful and picture perfect as many ideas may be, the caregiver support and guidance that are required are not always reflected in the same post. During the lockdown period, I noticed an increase in the number of very young children engaging in activities that were not developmentally appropriate, often influenced by an adult-led agenda. Again, the opportunity cost of children engaging in activities that are not developmentally appropriate is that they miss out on the play opportunities that their growing bodies and minds need.

In this section, I am not going to list all the milestones between birth and six but will rather provide a short description of the play stages and main focus areas during these periods. Refer back to these play stages and play development, as discussed in chapter 1, and reflect on whether the play materials and play space support your child in their play stage. I will be referring to the work of Takata (1974) as I describe the different play stages, or play epochs, as per her terminology. You will note that the skills build on each other throughout these stages.

The sensorimotor stage: 0–2 years

This play stage is characterised by the exploration of senses and body movements, objects and the environment around them. They are keen observers and imitators during this time as they learn more about themselves, their bodies and surrounding world. Repetitive play is often observed during this period, which can give caregivers an indication of the child's current play interests (see more on play schemas previously discussed). They will adapt their play as skills become easier, adjusting the challenge as they go. Pretend play actions may be observed from 12–18 months onwards, as they imitate and re-enact events in their routine with which they are familiar. Unoccupied play (focused on their body and body movements) is mostly observed during the first year of life, extending to solitary play and play with a close caregiver, such as a parent or primary caregiver.

Play prompts and the play space should focus on providing opportunities for:

- Emotional connection and imitation with a close caregiver.
- Discovering and exploring their senses and body movements.
- Exploring object properties.
- Practising new motor skills.
- Simple problem solving.
- Exploring cause and effect.
- Simple pretend play actions (around the one-year mark).

Mouthing is an important consideration during this stage, as mouthing helps children to learn about objects, their size, texture and so on. This behaviour usually starts decreasing around 18 months, but you may continue to see this up until the age of approximately two years. Children start exploring more with their fingers between the ages of two and three years.

Safety considerations, including the size and make-up of play materials, are important. Provide play materials that are safe and non-toxic. Model desired behaviours and teach which objects or items do not belong in their mouths, while providing them with suitable alternatives. The aim should not be to limit mouthing up to two years, but rather to offer safe exploration to ensure that their sensory needs are met, with caregiver supervision.

 You can use the toilet roll test to make sure that the item will not pose a choking hazard. Take a play prompt and see if it fits through a toilet roll. If it fits through, children up to and including three years of age should not be left unsupervised with that play prompt, as the whole object can fit into their mouth posing a choking hazard.

In this play stage, play is focused on exploration, discovery and experimentation. Repetition allows them to build neural connections, construct knowledge and make meaning of their surrounding world. You will notice a shift from babies who initially explore an object's properties to toddlers who want to understand what the object can do or what they can do with the object.

There are many options for objects for them to explore at this stage, from placing a mirror, large sensory ball or even a Tupperware or cup in front of them during tummy time for them to explore and manipulate, to giving them a treasure basket with a whisk and play silk stuck inside, textured balls, etc. once they become proficient at sitting. To offering safe, large, loose parts with different textures that can be moved and manipulated by one- to two-year olds as they stack, push things over or pour water with funnels and cups as part of water play. Taking their sensory needs (how much input they need and can manage), developmental skills and play interests into consideration will build on their free play skills.

> Your little one is starting to develop their attention span from around 10 months of age. Typical attention span ranges from approximately three to five minutes per year of a child's age. Be realistic with your expectations when it comes to free play. Free play and attention span are skills that strengthen over time with exposure and stimulating play opportunities.

The symbolic and simple constructive stage: 2-4 years

In this play stage you will see a widening of their imaginary worlds, progress in their physicality and a growing interest in and ability to engage with and relate to others. Their pretend play extends from simple pretend actions to pretend sequences from their routines and life experiences. Symbolic play is observed through pretend actions with invisible or unconventional props, such as pouring pretend tea, serving a plate of cookies or answering a call on a wooden block as their cell phone. Their symbolic play skills will continue to develop throughout the preschool years. They enjoy building and creating simple constructions that represent other objects or situations that may be used as part of their play exchange, such as building a farm and using figurines to re-enact a farm outing. There is a shift from parallel play (playing next to others) to more engagement between playmates towards the latter part of this play stage, but not yet the organisation or group direction that will be observed in the following stage.

Open-ended toys and objects that can grow with your child and be used in various ways as part of their play throughout these three stages include:	Let's not forget things around the home:
<ul><li>Wooden blocks and slats or other types of construction sets e.g. magnetic tiles</li><li>Play silks or scarves</li><li>Wooden rocker board or wobble board</li><li>Rainbow stacker</li><li>Figurines, such as animals and peg people</li><li>Wooden rings and wooden coins</li><li>Dolls</li><li>Transportation vehicles</li></ul>	<ul><li>Boxes</li><li>Washing baskets</li><li>Cushions and pillows (and perhaps other pieces of furniture that get mom's okay)</li><li>Bed sheets or blankets</li><li>Parent's old clothes</li><li>Nature play</li></ul>

Play prompts and the play space should focus on providing opportunities for:
- Physicality, both for larger muscle group development and inner body senses (vestibular and proprioception).
- Exploration and involvement of all sensory systems.
- Creative expression using various art materials, focusing on the process not the end product.
- Construction with open-ended materials.
- Symbolic play with open-ended materials and props.
- Emotional connection with others.
- Ongoing development of self-regulation skills.
- Development of executive functioning skills.

The dramatic complex constructive and pre-game stage: 4-7 years

During this play stage there is more cooperation between playmates as their social participation and skills expand. Gross and fine motor skills are refined throughout this stage. Their symbolic play involves dramatic role play with scripts, which may be reality and/or fantasy based. They are able to design complex constructions as their various cognitive, problem solving and visuo-spatial skills strengthen throughout this stage.

Play prompts and the play space should focus on providing opportunities for:

- Physicality, both for larger muscle group development and inner body senses (vestibular and proprioception).
- Exploration and involvement of all sensory systems.
- Creative expression through various art materials and a continued refinement of fine motor skills.
- More complex construction play, with open-ended materials.
- Symbolic play, with open-ended materials that allow for roles, scripts and sequences of events as part of the play engagement.
- Establishing emotional connections with others.
- Ongoing development of self-regulation skills.
- Development of executive functioning skills.

The above stages aim to remind caregivers of important developmental and play stage considerations. Within each of these different play stages, children will display varying play interests that provide insights into their inner motivations. These are important considerations in choosing developmentally appropriate play prompts that further spark their interest and allow them to become fully immersed in their free play.

PLAY INTEREST CONSIDERATIONS

To support free play, it is important to observe and reflect on children's intrinsic play motivations, i.e. what they enjoy and what they seek out through play. By tuning in and observing the actions or games your little one repeats and attempts to persist at until they achieve mastery, will provide you with insight into their inner play motivation/s.

To support a deep, sustained focus in free play, child agency and motivation are key. As I mentioned in chapter 3, *The Child at Play*, this is not limited to particular play themes, such as farm animals, the ocean, fairies or dinosaurs, but, in particular for younger children, also include play schemas that you may often observe.

Listed on the next few pages are a few ideas to spark play based on play schemas… the list of play materials you can provide is limitless.

CONNECTING AND DISCONNECTING PLAY SCHEMAS

THINK OF THINGS THAT:	PROVIDE THE FOLLOWING TO SUPPORT AND EXPAND THEIR PLAY SCHEMA:
<ul><li>Construct or deconstruct</li><li>Can be built or taken apart</li><li>Join or separate</li><li>Can stretch</li><li>Are rigid</li><li>Are fragile</li><li>Are strong</li><li>Can be tied</li><li>Are removable</li><li>Can be cut</li></ul>	<ul><li>Construction prompts, e.g. wooden blocks, Lego, Duplo, magnetic tiles or wooden tracks</li><li>Strings or thread</li><li>Nuts and bolts</li><li>Magnets, magnetic wands and magnetised items (perhaps a mix of magnetised and non-magnetised for discovery)</li><li>PVC pipes and connectors</li><li>Different sizes of boxes for stacking and pushing over</li><li>Things to glue or stick</li><li>Items for peeling fruits or vegetables</li><li>Scissors for snipping grass, leaves and small sticks as part of outdoor play (supervision with scissors and other manipulative tools may be required)</li></ul>

ENCLOSING, CONTAINING AND ENVELOPING PLAY SCHEMAS

THINK OF THINGS THAT:	PROVIDE THE FOLLOWING TO SUPPORT AND EXPAND THEIR PLAY SCHEMA:
<ul><li>Can be wrapped</li><li>Can be hidden</li><li>Are visible/invisible</li><li>Can be climbed in/out of</li><li>The child can be inside/outside of</li><li>They can be under/over</li><li>Can be filled/emptied</li></ul>	<ul><li>Small tent or fort space</li><li>Bags, purses, shoe boxes, suitcases, tins, wallets, baskets, boxes, buckets, bowls and so on</li><li>Towel, blanket, pieces of fabric, play silks, scarves and so on</li><li>Posting toys</li><li>Nesting toys</li><li>Role play items, such as cloaks, bandages, hats and other materials that can be used to wrap themselves or items</li><li>Construction sets that can be used for creating fences, with animal figurines</li></ul>

TRAJECTORY, RADIAL AND ROTATION PLAY SCHEMAS

THINK OF THINGS THAT:	PROVIDE THE FOLLOWING TO SUPPORT AND EXPAND THEIR PLAY SCHEMA:
<ul><li>Fly</li><li>Spin</li><li>Float</li><li>Go up</li><li>Fall</li><li>Drop</li><li>Go down</li><li>Are slow</li><li>Are fast</li><li>Bounce</li><li>Twirl</li><li>Go around</li></ul>	While you may need boundaries at mealtime with regards to throwing food, consider how and where you can allow them to explore the movement of self and objects. Again, if you are concerned inside, take it outside or include it as part of bath time. Provide a space where they can throw or roll different items, toys and weights and see how far or how fast some items go or how big a splash something makes. Some ideas for objects you can provide them with: <ul><li>Balls of different sizes, weights and textures</li><li>Nature play items, such as feathers, leaves or pebbles</li><li>Blowing bubbles</li><li>Slingshot, which could be homemade with them</li><li>Swing and jungle gym sets that allow for movement on different planes, such as seated, lying down, upside down or spinning in different positions</li><li>A busy board with different knobs from old appliances, gears, cogs, nuts and bolts that can be rotated</li><li>Bottles with twisting caps</li><li>Toys with wheels or tires</li><li>Toy cars and ramps with a wobble board, a box or some other recycled items</li><li>Marbles</li><li>Wands, play silks, scarves or ribbons on sticks that can twirl or spin (especially on a windy day)</li><li>Whisks, funnels and so on for water play</li></ul>

BOUNDARIES PLAY SCHEMA

THINK OF THINGS THAT:	PROVIDE THE FOLLOWING TO SUPPORT AND EXPAND THEIR PLAY SCHEMA:
<ul><li>The child can go through</li><li>The child or object can be inside or outside of</li><li>That are big and/or small</li></ul>	<ul><li>Rainbow stackers and other construction materials</li><li>Tunnels or boxes</li><li>Items to post</li><li>Funnels or PVC pipes for water and sand play</li><li>Marble runs</li></ul>

ORIENTATION OR PERSPECTIVE PLAY SCHEMA

THINK OF THINGS THAT:	PROVIDE THE FOLLOWING TO SUPPORT AND EXPAND THEIR PLAY SCHEMA:
<ul><li>Go up/down</li><li>Go forwards/backwards</li><li>Can be near/far</li><li>Go upside down/upright</li><li>They can be on top/underneath of</li></ul>	<ul><li>Provide opportunities to swing in various positions, e.g. seated, or on their tummy, or go down the slide in different ways, e.g. lying down or lying on their tummy, and to climb back up</li><li>Allow for opportunities to climb up trees, Pikler triangles, climbing frames and jungle gyms, and time for them to relax and enjoy the view from the top... as they notice how things look smaller when they are higher up</li><li>Mats for rolling or playing on their tummy</li><li>Toilet rolls for pretend binoculars that they can peep through</li><li>Kaleidoscopes or magnifying glasses, which they can use to enlarge items or insects</li></ul>

POSITIONING OR ORDERING PLAY SCHEMA

THINK OF THINGS THAT:	PROVIDE THE FOLLOWING TO SUPPORT AND EXPAND THEIR PLAY SCHEMA:
<ul><li>They can be inside/outside of</li><li>They can be under/on top of</li><li>They can be behind/in front of</li><li>They can be in between</li><li>Are different colours, shapes, sizes or weights</li><li>Are the same/different</li><li>Can stack/unstack</li><li>They can balance</li></ul>	Lining up, sorting or classifying can likely be done with many materials and play prompts that you already have in your home, or can be found in nature. If you notice that they enjoy this, you can set out a mixed box of animals or other figurines, vehicles, balls of different sizes, Grapat sets or construction sets. Out and about, it may be exploring pebbles of different sizes, leaves or the lengths of the sticks they pick up.

TRANSFORMING PLAY SCHEMA

THINK OF THINGS THAT:	PROVIDE THE FOLLOWING TO SUPPORT AND EXPAND THEIR PLAY SCHEMA:
<ul><li>Can mix</li><li>Have different textures</li><li>Can freeze/melt</li><li>Are dry/wet</li></ul>	<ul><li>Mud kitchen</li><li>Water and sand</li><li>Painting to experiment with mixing colours or engaging in creative art play</li><li>Items for cooking or baking</li></ul>

TRANSPORTING PLAY SCHEMA

THINK OF THINGS THAT:	PROVIDE THE FOLLOWING TO SUPPORT AND EXPAND THEIR PLAY SCHEMA:
<ul><li>Can move</li><li>Can go in/out of something</li><li>Can be emptied/filled</li><li>Can be open/closed</li></ul>	<ul><li>Bags, purses, shoe boxes, suitcases, tins, wallets, baskets, boxes, buckets, bowls and so on</li><li>Scoops, spades, droppers, syringes, spoons, bottles, jugs, etc.</li><li>Push trolleys, prams or wheelbarrows</li><li>Diggers, tractors and dumpers, as part of nature play</li><li>Pulleys</li><li>Kitchen play sets</li></ul>

OTHER PLAY SCHEMAS: EG. SOUND

THINK OF THINGS THAT:	PROVIDE THE FOLLOWING TO SUPPORT AND EXPAND THEIR PLAY SCHEMA:
<ul><li>Shake</li><li>Bang</li><li>Rattle</li><li>Are loud/soft</li></ul>	<ul><li>Musical toys</li><li>Household items or recycled items that make different sounds, e.g. cylindrical gift wrap centres or PVC pipes</li></ul>

With regards to play themes, such as dinosaurs, transport and so on, including books on the topic, figurines, dress-up props, objects, items or props that link to the theme, construction materials and other open-ended materials as part of your *yes space* can help them embark on various play adventures.

PLAY SPACES AND PLAY PROMPTS

The *yes space*, a concept made popular by Janet Lansbury and the RIE approach, is likely to look different from family to family. Although it is lovely to be inspired by beautiful play spaces online, there are practical considerations that each family unit needs to consider. A copy and paste approach may not always work. I want to start this section off with general considerations regarding a *yes space*. From there we will look at different play spaces and play prompts based on different play categories.

The 'yes' space

A *yes space* should not pose too many restrictions or be a space where children hear, 'No, don't do that', 'No, move away from there' or, 'No, you're too close to that.' Too many *no's* will affect the flow of play and the child's ability to engage in free play with confidence. We will discuss the *here and near dance* concept soon, but I do want to add here that, developmentally speaking, children who fall within the unoccupied, solitary and parallel play stages will require a play space in very close proximity to their main caregiver. The space should be close enough so that they can hear and see their caregiver to build on their capacity for free play. This closer proximity will also allow the caregiver to see the child for safety and supervision. Initially, the *yes space* may be a shared space in the main living area of the home. Later, the play space may move further away from the immediate sight of a caregiver, as they start playing more in their bedrooms, for example. Age mixing with siblings, or as part of a small playgroup, may result in younger children playing more confidently in play spaces that are not right next to their caregiver (with caregiver supervision as required based on the needs of the family unit).

A few points to consider:

- Which location or room will be a good play space in your home? Consider a space where you are close enough to engage in a *here and near dance* and offer safety supervision, especially with young children.
- Safety considerations, such as things that can fall over, on top of them, breakable items, electrical wiring and so on.
- Is the area or room free of distractions, such as screens that could potentially interrupt the flow of play?
- Sensory considerations, as per the discussion in The Child at Play chapter, see your child's particular play profile for more specific considerations. Is the space too noisy or visually distracting? How much natural light does the space have? Consider cooler, calmer colours versus bright colours.
- Accessibility and visibility of play prompts. Ideally low shelving should be used, but also consider low profile bins, baskets and containers so that they can independently access, combine and use play prompts. How high are the items? How heavy is the bin, basket or container? How large is the bin, basket or container? Constantly calling a caregiver to fetch or pass play prompts will interrupt the flow of play and their ability to engage in deep sustained play. Look at the set-up from their lower level and consider the ease of picking up and moving the containers, baskets, trays or bins based on their hand and arm size, not necessarily an adult's.

- Your *yes space* may combine the play spaces that we will discuss later. You may have different or separate play spaces for some of the play categories. You may have a corner in a communal living space with a play mat to indicate the separation between the living area and the play area, or you may have a separate playroom altogether. It depends on what works in your home, for your family unit, your children and you. However, ensure that there is a space dedicated to play.
- Be mindful of your child or children's ages, development and play stages and how these can impact on certain requirements for the *yes space*. For example, a 10-month-old baby's yes play space will look different to an older child's, with additional safety considerations and closer proximity to their main caregiver/s.
- Less means more play: fewer toys, less clutter and less visually overwhelming stimuli can ease a child's ability to process and decide on play prompts to use and combine. More toys do not equate to more play but can rather have the opposite effect.
- Does the play area have open space? Is the space cluttered or filled with furniture and play prompts, with limited open space to manipulate, combine and engage in play?

Play spaces should ideally allow children the opportunity to engage in and carry their play interests or play themes across various play categories. Play areas can be fluid and may tap into various play categories simultaneously if careful consideration has been given to the setup and inclusion of play prompts in the play area. The aim of this section is to make you mindful, to allow for observation and reflection on your play space as to whether it allows for play engagement across play categories.

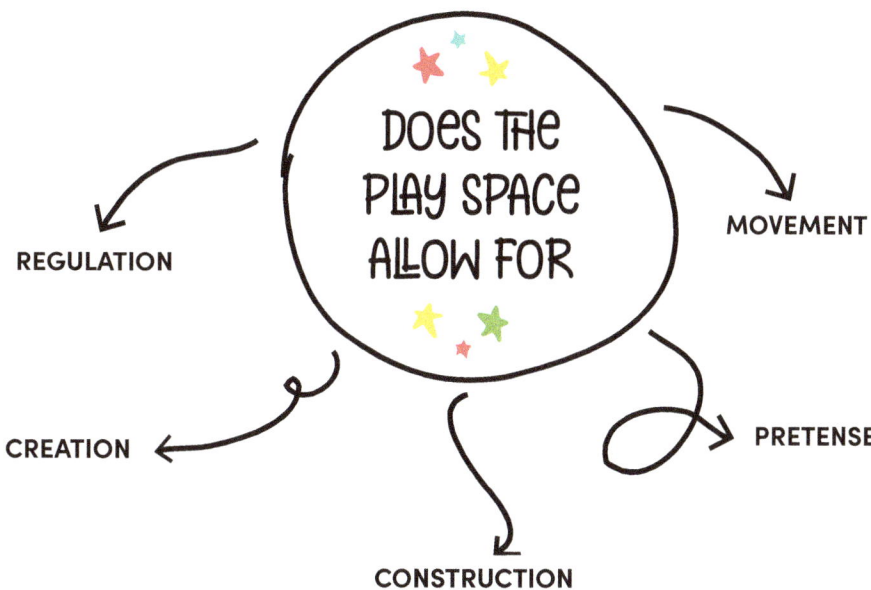

Figure 10: Play Spaces

Movement play space

Does your play area allow for movement? Do you have indoor and/or outdoor play spaces that afford different play opportunities and movement experiences? This certainly will depend on the size of your home or apartment and the availability of space. However, even in smaller apartments, movement can be included, perhaps with more careful consideration, by using boxes or washing baskets that can be pulled and pushed, obstacle courses with furniture, rocker or wobble boards, pickler sets and so on.

The importance of movement in play is not limited to strengthening postural components and gross motor development only, but also provide the vestibular and proprioception senses with input to strengthen our *inner body map*, while also having a regulating effect. Children often intrinsically know what sensory experiences their bodies need. If the surrounding play context supports them, they are able to access play opportunities through free play that are in line with their sensory needs. Furthermore, movement opportunities and risky play allow children to engage in motor planning and tap into their executive functioning skills, to only name a few of the many benefits! Movement play can merge with one or more of the other play spaces.

Movement play prompts can include, but are certainly not limited to:

- Trees and natural play spaces.
- Jungle gym apparatus.
- Loose outdoor play parts, such as tires, planks, crates, large boxes, ropes and other recycled materials.
- Outside pulleys.
- Rocker and wobble boards.
- Pickler triangles, slides and climbing frame sets.
- Wooden rocking boats and climbing frames.
- Tunnels.
- Carts, scooters and bicycles.
- Indoor and outdoor swings, such as hammock swings, tire swings and spandex swings.
- Cushions, pillows and other (approved) pieces of home furniture.

These are only a few examples. From trees to boxes to rocker boards, the possibility of movement input is all around us.

Pretend play space

Pretend play can certainly merge and occur in combination with other play categories. I would like to add here that pretend play can occur in both a child dressing up and becoming a character or taking on a role as well as manipulative pretend play, where they may direct a smaller scene using figurines and manipulatives. Therefore, this can allow a merging of pretend, movement, construction and creative play, as they engage in their play adventure while tapping into various developmental skills.

Pretend play prompts can include, but are certainly not limited to:

- Dress up props, items and costumes, including fantasy characters, old, donated clothing items, a hat and handbag grandma is no longer using, a tie from dad and so on.
- Animal figurines, peg people, dolls and more.
- Play silks or scarves.
- Wooden blocks, Duplo, Lego, magnetic tiles and other construction sets.
- Rainbow stackers, rectangular stackers and semi-circle stackers.
- Larger sets such as a kitchenette or doll house but also large boxes.
- Musical instruments and toys.
- Storybooks.
- Loose parts from around the home, such as Tupperware, funnels, cups, etc.
- Loose parts from recycling, such as bottle caps, toilet rolls, gift wrap rolls, etc.
- Loose parts from nature, such as pebbles, leaves, sticks, etc.
- Loose parts that can be bought, such as wooden rings, pom poms, wooden coins, Grapat and more.

The ability to combine some of the above mentioned items can set little ones off on many wonderful play adventures.

Construction play space

Construction, pretend and movement play may often merge. You should carefully consider play prompts that are versatile, allowing the same item to be used in various ways and as part of different play categories.

Construction play prompts can include, but are certainly not limited to:

- Wooden blocks, Duplo, Lego, magnetic tiles and other construction sets.
- Train tracks or Waytoplay road sets.
- Rainbow stackers, rectangular stackers and semi-circle stackers.
- Loose parts from around the home, such as Tupperware, funnels, cups, etc.
- Loose parts from recycling, such as boxes, toilet rolls, gift wrap rolls and other packing material, to name only a few.
- Loose parts from nature, such as pebbles, leaves, sticks, etc.
- Loose parts that can be bought, such as wooden rings, pom poms, wooden coins, Grapat and more.

Creation play space

Does your play space allow for creative expression? I am not referring to art kits or copy-this-craft activities. I am talking about creative expression, where the focus is process rather than product driven. There appears to have been a shift, an increase in arts and crafts that focus on copying or replicating an adult-made, pre-made example, rather than providing children with craft and art materials and allowing them to explore and expand on their own play interests. Creative play is more than strengthening hand components and fine motor skills. It can involve various senses by using different scents or textured materials, and it can tap into visuo-spatial and motor planning skills as the child works out how to make their bird or dinosaur out of toilet roll, play dough, leaves and more.

The child's age will be an important consideration when deciding which materials can be left out permanently, and which materials and items the caregiver will bring out and remain in close proximity to monitor while the child engages with them. The advantage of always having certain creative materials out and accessible is that they can use the materials to expand their play, such as designing a sign for their shop, a flag for their ship and so on. This allows them to add to their play as their play adventure evolves. A deeper focus and more intrinsically motivated engagement can occur when they draw, create and design as part of their play theme.

You may have a set up with a small table and chairs and a tray that can be easily placed, lifted, wiped and cleaned, or you may choose to do creative play in the bathroom or outside.

Creative play prompts can include, but are certainly not limited to:

- Paper, cardboard, scissors, crayons, paint, glue, pom poms, ribbons and various other art and craft supplies.
- Playdough (scented play dough can add a wonderful additional sensory element, as well as having a regulating effect, in particular calmer smells, such as lavender or vanilla).
- Cloud dough, kinetic sand or various other slimes or sand mixtures that can be made with ingredients found in the home.
- Natural materials, such as pebbles, sticks, feathers, leaves and more.
- Recycled materials, such as bottle caps, toilet rolls, packaging material and more.
- Easels (canvas, white board, chalk board or Perspex), small table and chairs, containers and trays.
- Books can serve as wonderful inspiration to page through while they draw, paint or create (although you may need to consider placement to avoid pages being glued together during creative pursuits).

Regulation play space

Does your play space allow for regulation? As I mentioned earlier, varying bucket sizes may need varying amounts and type of sensory stimuli. Movement, deep pressure and heavy muscle work opportunities play an important regulatory role in managing bucket levels and can be incorporated as part of a regulation space. The focus of the remainder of this section, however, will be on reflecting whether your play space allows a safe space to reset, to manage bucket levels and/or a bucket that has spilled over.

We all need some quiet or alone time every now and again... time and space to regulate and calm our sensory systems. Free play can assist with regulation IF the play space allows for this. Helping children to feel empowered to access, practise and learn self-regulation is an important (and often overlooked) life skill.

Create a quiet and calm corner or space, a place to retreat, which should ideally be in a quieter, less busy spot in your home or school and should be accessible at all times. Children do not yet have the language for or reflective capacity regarding self-regulation in the younger years. Their actions will often show what they need. Allowing them to access the quiet or calm space as and when they need it will give them the opportunity to learn self-regulation skills through an in-tune caregiver who can observe when they use the space and the affect it has on them. Co-regulation is still key. Although the regulation play space may sometimes be a part of a playroom, consider, for example, the impact of sibling play. One might like some quiet time in a tee-pee, while the other is on a roaring dinosaur adventure with exploding volcanoes and full sound effects right outside. Those differing play and sensory needs may lead to disagreements at times.

Regulation prompts can include, but are certainly not limited to:
- A small tent, tee-pee or self-made fort space using chairs, cushions and blankets or towels (enclosed spaces have a calming and regulating effect on the nervous system, as external stimuli are blocked out and a quieter, darker, and enclosed, womb-like space is created).
- Hammock or enclosed swing.

Also consider items that can be included inside the calm space, such as small pillows or cushions, a blanket, a few books, glow in the dark items or a lava lamp (especially if your little one may be scared of the dark), soft and scented items (lavender, vanilla or rose scents for example) and comfort toys.

A *regulation space* may be used differently on different days. It may form part of the play adventure, such as a cave, or they may simply want to snuggle up and page through a favourite book.

In the play spaces described above, we can see that play categories may often merge and occur in the same shared play space. Some play prompts afford versatility in that they can be used in many different ways as part of the various play categories.

We want to opt for play prompts that allow a child to think and be an active participant in their play, not to sit back and be entertained (often for a short amount of time) by the toy. How much does the play prompt do for your child versus how much can your child do with the play prompt?

Reflect on your use and inclusion of open-ended materials, including loose parts, as part of adult-led and structured activities compared to open-ended play. How much do you allow the child to do with the play prompt versus how much do you instruct in or place limits on their use? There is so much more to loose parts than sorting them into three colour groups, counting to ten or lining them up from big to small... here is where the adult agenda in play creeps in once again. Consider the balance between play and structured activities in your home. How much of it is play and how much is non-play?

Let's clarify a few concepts:

OPEN-ENDED PLAY

This refers to play that is not limited by expectations, outcomes or rules. This type of play is spontaneous and can unfold in many creative ways, as children choose how to explore, manipulate and combine the play materials as part of their play script. Their play engagement is intrinsically motivated, spontaneous, not limited by directives and not necessarily reality bound. There is no right or wrong way to play!

OPEN-ENDED PLAY MATERIALS

This refers to play prompts that allow children to make independent choices regarding their play actions and play scripts and support spontaneous, creative free play. These play prompts do not have set rules or directions regarding their use. A child can choose how to use, explore, manipulate and combine open-ended materials as part of their play adventure.

Open-ended materials include, but are not limited to, dolls, animal figurines, cars or other vehicles, characters, e.g. Lego people and/or peg people, wooden blocks, rainbow stackers, play silks, boxes and other packing materials, art materials and loose parts (see more on this below). These can be described as timeless toys, as they grow with a child. Play with open-ended materials will become more elaborate over time, from initially stacking wooden blocks as a baby to building a castle as a pre-schooler.

In comparison, close-ended toys have specific rules associated with their use, often teach a specific skill and have a clear end point to work towards, for example, shape sorters or puzzles. Children will outgrow the toy once they develop the particular skill associated with it.

LOOSE PARTS

Loose parts is a term coined by architect Simon Nicholson. This refers to items that can be moved, combined, put together, pulled apart and, in other words, used in many different ways. These items are non-prescriptive and non-specific and appear to have no apparent play purpose. Loose parts allow children to play in endless creative ways, without their play being dictated by the actual properties of the items.

The categories of loose parts can include:

- Items from nature, such as pebbles, feathers, sticks, shells and so on.
- Items from around the home, such as cups, plastic containers, funnels, jugs, utensils and many more.
- Items from recycling, such as toilet rolls, boxes, egg cartons, gift wrap rolls and other packaging materials.
- Items and toys that can be bought, such as wooden blocks, wooden rings, craft supplies, such as pom poms, buttons, etc.

PLAY PROMPT VERSATILITY

Within open-ended play materials, some play prompts afford higher play versatility than others. For example, a doll can be included in different play sequences and scripts, e.g. feeding baby, bathing baby, putting baby to bed, taking baby for a visit to the doctor and so on. In all these instances, the baby will be a baby. The same can be said of a Lego driver. The driver may have different roles, such as driving to school, fetching groceries or becoming an uber driver, but it will still be a Lego driver.

In comparison, a wooden block can be used as a cell phone, car or part of a castle. Peg people can represent a man, woman, child, astronaut, driver, chef, princess, fairy or any character a child chooses to assign. These open-ended materials afford higher play versatility than a doll or Lego driver, for example.

Two aspects to consider regarding high versus low play versatility:

- Can the object, toy or item be used in a variety of ways during play, rather than having one sole role or use?
- The longevity of the same toy or object across the age groups. In other words, can the same toy or object be played with in different ways as the child grows.

INVITATION TO PLAY

This involves setting up developmentally appropriate play materials, in line with a child's play interest/s and without instruction or particular end goal in mind, in other words, no right or wrong outcome. We will cover more on this as part of the strategies to support free play.

A few considerations about play prompts:
- Consider whether the play prompts are developmentally appropriate and in line with current play interests.
- Quality over quantity. As per earlier discussions, play spaces that are too cluttered and include too many play prompts can overwhelm children, making it difficult for them to process and formulate play ideas. Studies have found that children play for longer and more deeply with fewer toys, not more!
- The ratio of open-ended to closed-ended toys and play prompts within the play space/s.
- Limiting the number of battery-operated toys.
- High versus low play versatility with regards to open-ended play materials.
- Out of sight is often out of mind. That is why you may, at times, see a sudden strong attachment to a toy or item that you are putting aside for charity or to give to a family member or friend, as it sparks a renewed interest. Toy rotation helps to spark excitement and novelty when they see the item/s in the play space once again.
- Family play spaces may include family or shared play prompts as opposed to *my* or *your* toys.
- Some children may require grading of open-ended materials to develop their skill and confidence. As part of play development, children often initially use miniature versions of real-life items, such as a small pot, pan or a wooden car. Some children may require grading to move from replicated real life play prompts to unconventional or more open-ended materials.
- You may initially grade the items so that they resemble the shape and/or colour of the real-life item. For example, a red ball that represents an apple or a round container lid that represents a plate, later moving onto leaves and pebbles or mandala pieces used as a pretend range of fruits and vegetables, thereby developing their ability to engage with open-ended materials and loose parts through grading and exposure.
- Play is not only momentary. Some children may see a play script through over days or even weeks. Consider a *to be continued* tray or table for play adventures that they may wish to carry over. Each family unit may have different rules regarding clean up and keeping and breaking up of creations, particularly if other siblings or peers wish to have a turn with the play prompts later.
- Mouthing of objects typically decreases from around 18 months, with the behaviour still noted until approximately two years of age, as they start exploring more with their fingers between two and three years of age. It is important to consider the size and safety of play prompts that a child can play with unsupervised, until the age of three. This refers to the size and the material (e.g. whether the paint used is non-toxic).

- Additional considerations for the use and storage of play prompts may be required in families or schools with children of varying ages. Older children may play with items that could be seen as choking hazards for younger children. If this is the case, consider the play prompts used in communal play spaces.

I want to add here that there is not necessarily one magic play prompt that will elicit hours of free play. Some open-ended materials and loose parts toys may be left sitting pretty on shelves. They will do nothing if they are not developmentally appropriate or well matched to your child's play interests. Open-ended play is a skill that will develop, and it may be necessary to grade, as discussed above, or present materials in ways that show the child the potential and the varying ways that the item can be incorporated into their play.

PLAY AESTHETICS

In concluding our section on play prompts and play spaces, I want to ask, what does play look like? What does a play space look like? Is it always picture perfect and Instagram worthy? Probably not. Play is not always pretty or picture perfect. It is not meant to be. An overfocus on the look of play may cause us to lose the critical importance of the process of play. Play is about the process, the play adventure, the journey. If you haven't been able to catch the perfect play moments for an Instagram Story, relax! Play is in the eye of the beholder, as Sutton-Smith (1997) says, and boy oh boy, can it take on some interesting forms! The value of play does not lie in the picture-perfect play post; it lies in the giggles, the smiles, the, 'I did it!' triumphant moments, the dinosaur roars and pirate 'Arrrhs', the fairy dances and magic potions, the made-up songs and character names and the pure joy and exuberance that is play.

 "We want to move away from serving the I'm bored culture to nurturing the I'm bored space, from directing every aspect of play to supporting play."

SUPPORTING FREE PLAY ENGAGEMENT

Depending on a child's age, play stage and play skills different strategies and tips will be more applicable than others. As we discussed in *play development*, a caregiver will be a baby and toddler's first playmate and, in many ways, a play mentor during the early play years. During these early play years, caregivers can already start developing the child's capacity for free play and continue to support play as they grow.

Some children may need additional support strategies, owing to individual differences, even when a caregiver has put special thought and consideration into the play space setup and play prompt selection.

Children will build on their capacity for and the duration of free play over time, with exposure and opportunity. Don't necessarily expect a three-hour free play slot the first time you trial new strategies but consider their age, attention span, play stage and mood on the day. Some children may simply need to be given the time and opportunity to become captains of their own play adventures, rather than play being a strictly scheduled event. Scheduling a fifteen-minute free play slot between lunch and the next extra mural does not allow them to become fully immersed in their play. I have written the remainder of this chapter in a question-and-answer style, based on questions I have often received on the topic of supporting free play.

What if my child always wants me to play with them?

First, as we discussed earlier in the book, children who feel secure will be more likely to engage independently in free play. Neediness in play may be due to other emotional needs that you should consider. For children who have been used to an adult presence in their play for a period of time, consider introducing free play after spending quality time together and using my here and near dance principle below.

The PlayMore here and near dance

When children are younger, we want to ensure that they feel safe and confident with the idea of playing and exploring. Remember that, based on different developmental play stages and age ranges, children will initially require a play space in close proximity to their main caregiver. The here and near dance will be applied differently depending on your child's age and the extent of the habit that has been created of you being their full-time playmate. The idea is, **we are not leaving them alone, but leaving the play alone.**

In a gentle way, we are handing over the ownership of their play to them. The rhythm of your here and near dance may be different with each child. Some may need a slower rhythm, you checking in and encouraging a bit more often, where others may respond well and become so involved with the flow of their play that they can happily play by themselves for a period of time. It is about tuning in to your child on the day and supporting the flow of their free play.

Initially, especially if a child has been used to having you as a full-time playmate, it may require that you engage with them at the start and then, during parts of the play engagement, being close enough that they can hear or see you in the room, but not necessarily hovering over them.

To slip out of the play engagement, without ending the game or play script altogether, you may need to consider the role you step into at the start of the play engagement. Choose a role or character that will potentially have a smaller role. Don't be the king to the queen or vice versa. Be a supporting character that can come in, have a few lines and gently go off while the main characters continue.

For example, you could say, 'Okay, I will be the teddy. Ooh teddy looks sleepy to me. I think teddy is going to have one cup of tea (or one slice of cake or one cookie) and go to bed while you look after the rest of the guests.' Then engage in the play exchange, have a cup of tea or a delicious cookie, let teddy say goodnight to everyone and say, 'Enjoy the party everyone, I am off to nap. See you all again tomorrow,' and you gently move off to the side, out of the play scene, handing the ownership of the play to the child, shifting from the here in the play script to being nearby. The rhythm may require a here, near and here again, if the habit of playing with an adult full-time is very engrained. You may encourage by saying, 'Teddy still looks very tired and is dreaming away. I have few things to do while he sleeps but will be close by,' should they repeatedly request, 'Teddy to wake up.'

Consider the expectations you create prior to the play engagement. If you say, 'Yes, I will play with you,' this may indicate to them that you will be part of the play engagement from start to finish, versus saying, 'Yes, I will play with you for a few minutes and then I need to go check on your sister.' or, 'Yes, I will help you with the corners of the puzzle and then I need to start dinner and will come see your progress on the puzzle.' Here, near and then here again. Gradually, over time, you will decrease the here time and increase the near time, while expanding on their ability to be more independent during free play.

How do I join my child's play?

It is important to consider how to join in, and not unintentionally redirect, a child's play, as well as stepping away with minimal disruption to the flow of their play.

To ease the process of joining in your child's play, pick up a toy or object that closely relates to the play that they are engaged in and get down to their level. Don't try to change or redirect the play. Remember, you stepped into their inner play world, and this may make them feel that their idea or play game isn't good enough for you to play along with.

If you are struggling to mimic their play, or you feel unsure of the play script, your role or the sequence of events, ask a few questions such as, 'Tell me more about', 'Wow who is this?' or, 'Where are we going?' to gain an understanding of their inner play world, especially if you're not entirely sure if you entered a zoo, Jurassic Park, or if Elsa and Anna are visiting a farm that breeds dinosaurs. Don't ask too many questions or talk too much. Balance gaining a deeper insight into the game with allowing the play to flow without unnecessary interruptions.

If you can't stay for the full duration of the game and you wanted one-on-one time for connection with your little one but need to work or get dinner ready, as I mentioned earlier, enter as a supporting cast member, not a main character. That way, you can slowly introduce your exit with minimal disruption to the flow of their game.

How do I make sure I don't take the fun out of free play?

In instances where you join in free play, whether playing zoo or visiting their pretend restaurant, be aware of the adult agenda, turning it into a mini-lesson and taking the fun out of it, such as, 'Can you count how many cups you have in the kitchen?', 'How many cups are red and how many cups are blue?' Turning it into a stock count may result in the chef leaving and taking on a new job elsewhere.

Change the way you engage, as free play is full of wonderful learning opportunities, such as saying, 'Wow that cookie was delicious. I'm so hungry, could you please give me five more?', 'Red is my favourite colour, can I have a red plate for dinner please?' or, 'What's teddy's favourite colour? We can put that plate down for him.' During these interactions, we are still counting and identifying colours, but it fits within their play theme and maintains the fun. You'll be surprised at how much more they take in, learn and discover through these playful interactions than when you make it a mini lesson.

What if my child can't choose what to play?

After providing play prompts, allow time and opportunity for their play idea to develop. Don't be too quick to offer your own ideas. Offer encouragement and support, but limit the number of questions early on, as they may become discouraged and feel overwhelmed when bombarded with questions while they are trying to look around, process and formulate an idea. Remember, children's processing speed will develop over time and it is not the same as yours.

Try a *wait and see then respond, wait and see then respond* approach.

If after a few minutes you notice your child is still walking up and down (also see ideas on jump-starting play, *invitation to play* and toy rotation later on), cue with two options that aren't too specific so that they can still formulate their own idea. For example, 'Do you want to play with the blocks or with the animals?' Allow them time to think and make a choice instead of simply telling them what to use and how to use it. We want to avoid giving a specific idea and instruction, such as, 'Why don't you build a house?' You may even notice them combining the two options as they start to play.

'I'm bored'. How do I help my child to jump-start play?

We want to move away from serving the I'm bored culture to nurturing the I'm bored space, from directing every aspect of play to supporting play. Caregivers may support little ones by offering a bridge, a jump-start to move from the I'm bored space to playful engagement.

Let's move away from jumping onto your Pinterest board to set up various activities the moment you hear, 'I'm bored.' Learn how to help them navigate from the I'm bored space to playful engagement. Some children may want to retreat to a comfort zone, such as screen time, when boredom strikes. We are going to have a look at the *invitation to play* concept, toy rotation and inspiration cues.

INVITATION TO PLAY

The invitation to play concept originally derived from the Reggio Emilia philosophy and is deeply rooted in their approach to early childhood education. The Reggio Emilia philosophy offers children materials to explore, in a non-directive and creative manner, through which children lead their own learning while their teachers skilfully guide and support the process.

You may wonder, why the quick history detour? The #invitationtoplay on social media is not always what it seems. While the Reggio Emilia approach is intentional in the materials that are presented, the manner they are presented and the adult's role in the process, many #invititationtoplay posts lack child agency and an open-ended outcome as part of the process.

Some #invitationtoplay posts, on closer inspection, reveal that the adult has set up a structured activity, with very specific rules and a particular correct or incorrect end result. This is not play. If you want to jump-start play, free play, that end goal should be kept in the back of your mind.

INVITATION TO PLAY VERSUS INVITATION TO WORK

Providing a child with materials and exact instructions as to how materials should be manipulated and used is NOT an *invitation to play*. It is a structured activity. This does not help to bridge the I'm bored space or develop confidence in their free play. This occupies them until they meet the very specific end-goal, as dictated by the adult, and then the activity is over. This will reinforce the notion that they need an adult to tell them what to do, how to do it and for how long, whenever they feel boredom creeping up. This does not empower them to create magic out of the I'm bored space.

INVITATION TO PLAY VERSUS INVITATION TO WATCH

It shouldn't take you hours to set up an *invitation to play*. Setting up the most beautiful *invitation to play* should not be an online contest. If anything, the value does not lie in how beautiful the set-up is, but rather in the exploration and joy it brings your child, in the play adventures that it inspires and the minutes or hours of play that it ignites. It should invite children to play, manipulate and explore the pieces, NOT to watch it or play around it without breaking it. Don't restrict your little one's play by creating an elaborate piece of art that can't be touched, where you ended up doing a whole lot and they end up doing very little.

SETTING UP AN INVITATION TO PLAY AS A JUMP-START FOR FREE PLAY

Now that I have had the opportunity to air a few #invitationtoplay details, let's have a look at how to jump-start free play using the *invitation to play* concept. An *invitation to play* involves providing developmentally appropriate play materials in line with your child's play interest/s, without instructions or right or wrong criteria for success. This should inspire play that is linked to one of your little one's current play interest/s, should be quick to set up and should not be completed by the adult.

Some examples of items to set up an *invitation to play* are:

- If your little one is interested in trajectory: a ball and a few empty bottles.
- If your little one is interested in transporting: an empty box or washing basket and a few loose items around it.
- If your little one is interest in exploring and re-enacting parts of their daily routine: a play silk and a doll (not wrapped up) or a play silk, doll and an empty shoe box.
- If they are intrigued by a play theme focused on vehicles: a few wooden cars, wooden blocks and a wobble board.

An *invitation to play* is meant to inspire as they walk past the play space, to allow them to explore the play materials, to combine the play prompts according to their own play interests and, therefore, to direct their own play process and engagement. It should be a child-led experience.

The play may flow in a whole different direction than you initially thought while you were setting the items up. You may have set it up with a transport play theme in mind and suddenly the driver buys animals and starts a farm. Remember, the goal was to jump-start free play not to lead them to an exact end goal. If they use the materials in a different way than you intended or add different materials from the toy shelf, let the play flow in whatever direction they choose! If you add a particular expectation or try to steer it in a specific direction, it falls more towards an activity and less towards play. This may lead to frustration for both parties.

You don't have to offer a full set or collection, for example, the whole rainbow stacker or all twelve peg dolls. Mix and match between open-ended materials; it offers more variety. The *invitation to play* setup can demonstrate different ways to use the same item/s, for example, taking one piece of the rainbow stacker and placing it with cars and roads may result in the rainbow stacker piece being used as a bridge or two pieces could form a circle on the floor, with a play silk placed inside and animals off to the side, which could perhaps turn into a watering hole or a camp. The exposure to various presentations builds on their capacity to see the various potential uses of an item, which they may, over time, include more readily in their play repertoire.

To recap, a few tips for setting up an *invitation to play*:

- It should be quick to set up.
- Do not build a complete end result.
- Consider placing the play prompts on ground level rather than on top of shelves, this can be more inviting as they walk past.
- Do not try to take the lead or force an adult agenda onto the play engagement.
- Include open-ended and developmentally appropriate materials.
- Present materials in a manner that inspires the child to explore, combine and manipulate play prompts, with their play interest/s in mind.
- Allow the play to flow, even if it is not what you envisioned during the set up.

TOY ROTATION

Studies have found that when there are fewer play prompts in the child's play space, children:

- Engage in more free play.
- Have a deeper sustained focus and longer engagement.
- Become less overwhelmed during play.
- Come up with more inventive play ideas and play scripts.
- Use play prompts in interesting and unconventional ways.

Toy rotation not only helps to reduce clutter but also serves as a jump-start to free play by focusing on how the physical environment can impact play behaviour. There is no fixed time between rotations, this will be dependent on each child and their boredom cues and will differ between families.

Keep a few favourite play prompts out and rotate the remaining like-for-like items as part of collections, such as similar construction sets. Involve the *ringleader* and *magician* player profiles and try to make rotations a predictable experience, rather than a shock when they enter the play space the next day and are frantically searching for a loved item. Keep an eye out for an increase in boredom cues to indicate that it is time to rotate again. Try to take them saying, 'Again, again!' as a compliment that their neurons are doing a happy dance and firing away during their play. Do not rotate toys when you get bored of the repetition in their play but, again, look for their boredom cues instead.

COLLECT	CATEGORISE	COLLECTION	CHOOSE
• Collect all the toys and play prompts and decide what to keep, donate or use as out and about busy bags. • Compare the number of open-ended versus close-ended play prompts.	• Categorise like-for-like items, e.g. all construction sets. • Reflect: do you have items across all the play categories or only in one or two categories?	• Create collections that tap into the different categories, then mix and match. • Consider the different ages of siblings if they share a play space (items that can be used by siblings in their own unique ways). • The number of play prompts in a collection will vary depending on the ages and number of children you have.	• Choose which collection to display and which to store. • Choose a collection to be displayed at the child's eye level. Use low baskets and/or trays with play interest/s in mind. • Choose collection/s to be stored above the child's eye level or out of sight. • Observe if there are play prompts that remain unused while on display. • Rotate the collection when boredom cues increase.

INSPIRATION CUES

Try inspiration cues to jump-start play in moments of boredom. We want to be mindful of not giving them the answer, but rather supporting and nudging their ability to make a decision regarding their play, and how they are going to manage and spend their time in play and allowing them to practice autonomy in free play.

This may include:

- 'Hmm' or, 'I wonder?' cues, while being mindful of your child's age and the amount of specificity to include in your statement. Such as, 'Hmm, what could these blocks be?' instead of a too specific, 'Hmm, can you build an animal farm out of the blocks?' Grade the amount of specificity and detail you include and be mindful not to offer a complete solution or idea.
- Asking, 'What did you do the last time you were bored?'

You may use a combination of the jump-start strategies discussed above or, on occasion, you may only need to use one. You may need to use more with your one child, while your other child is able to engage in free play without additional jump-start cues. You may find yourself using more strategies initially and decreasing them over time as your child's confidence and free play skills develop. Identify and choose strategies based on your family and their specific play needs.

How do I support risky play?

This section will cover the concept of a risk analysis as part of physical play but could also be applied to play in general. We will also look at alternatives to saying, 'Be careful!'

First, caregivers need to distinguish between hazards and healthy challenges in play. The following quote from Sandseter's work on risky play captures this idea well:

"Adults should therefore try to eliminate hazards that children cannot see or manage without removing all risks, so that children are able to meet challenges and choose to take risks in relatively safe play settings. This means finding the balance between those risks that foster learning and the hazards that can result in serious injury."

– Sandseter, 2011, p. 261

For some caregivers, this will require reflection and thought to stop viewing every piece of jungle gym apparatus or tree as a hazard, but rather as a healthy play challenge. Most children (yes, there are children with specific play needs who struggle to regulate impulse control and may engage in excessive risk taking and therefore require additional support) tend to regulate risk in a gradual manner based on their own competence and their internal fear response. What I mean by this is that children tend to first climb one step and jump from there. They will repeat the process until they feel confident and then adjust the challenge by climbing to the next step and jumping from there. Most children won't climb to the highest point first and then jump from there. Children will often go a little higher each time, testing their capability. If they succeed, they will often repeat that level of challenge until they feel comfortable and capable of moving to the next challenge, thereby managing their risk during play opportunities that is both exciting and induces fear at times.

When it comes to risk analysis, caregivers need to consider environmental and child factors. With regard to child characteristics, age and skillset are important considerations. Each child will have their own skillset and capabilities in risky play. Peers and siblings may need varied challenges. Additional considerations may be required for children with additional needs, for example children with motor planning difficulties, sensory processing difficulties, ADHD or difficulties with impulse control and/or excessive risk-taking behaviours.

Environmental factors include:
- Features of the environment, e.g. is there a very busy road or is it fenced?
- Are there broken or missing parts to the playground equipment, tree or apparatus?
- Height, incline, difficulty and other factors, such as whether the playground equipment, tree or apparatus is dry or slippery.
- Is your child familiar with the playground equipment or apparatus, or is this their first time?

Caregivers who are aware of their child's capability and the surrounding context can help navigate and guide the degree of risk in risky play. Consider whether you suggest alternatives or adjustments, or do you simply avoid or limit risky play? Do you yell, 'Be careful!' every few seconds? Be careful of what, a snake, a ghost, a dinosaur?! It is not a very helpful or descriptive phrase to a child, is it?

Furthermore, too many 'Be careful!' and side-line commentaries can take away from your child's immediate focus, their body position and their grip and, instead, may lead to them looking up to you and your non-descriptive shout of, 'Be careful!' which can have the opposite effect altogether. Adults need to be mindful of when they choose to interfere in risky play and the information they provide. A poorly timed warning may contribute to the very slip you were worried about. Your warning can be void of meaning to a child. What exactly is it that this adult is warning me about?

I want to relate this to backseat driving, as a metaphor to describe what some children may be experiencing. Yes, my husband will certainly chuckle to himself when he reads this, as yes, I do provide occasional suggestions when he drives.

Imagine what it would feel like if someone were to warn you of every stop street, turn and traffic light on a road you frequently drive. If they are telling you step by step what to do, how and when to do it, that may leave you feeling that the other person does not have any faith in your driving abilities. If you are constantly sportscasting during play, and risky play in particular, you may be, unknowingly, sending messages that you do not trust in your child's abilities to play and to successfully (which isn't always achieved on the first attempt) manage the challenge.

It is only under certain circumstances that we may, for example, make a driver aware of an upcoming offramp, especially if they have not driven that road before. In that moment you wouldn't simply shout, 'Be careful!' or, 'Watch out!' which may give the driver a big fright, but you would rather gently suggest, 'Our offramp is coming up.' The latter is a more descriptive and useful statement for the driver in that instance.

Similarly, we want to offer well thought out, necessary feedback to children based on an adult's risk analysis of that particular play opportunity. Be intentional in allowing healthy challenges and risks, so that they can engage in their own risk analysis to become more proficient at risk management later on. Backseat driving minimises the learning opportunities that occur through a healthy dose of risky, or rather adventurous, explorative, physical play.

If you notice that they are stuck or that there is something you want to make them aware of, move away from saying, 'Be careful!' or, 'Watch out!' Rather use descriptive phrases that will scaffold and create an awareness of the environment, an awareness of themselves, an awareness of what to look out for in the future and an awareness of what makes something safe or unsafe, using cues that elicit problem solving and teach risk management, rather than doing it for them.

You can try out some of the following examples:

- Where will you put your foot?
- What can you use to get to the other side?
- What do you think will happen if…?
- Did you notice that the rocks are loose?
- Do you notice that the jungle gym is wet and slippery?
- What plan can you make to…?
- What is your plan for…?
- What do you think you can do next?

Engage in a process of risk management WITH your child, not FOR them.

"I hope that we, as a society, are able to reflect on the role of adults in nurturing and supporting play, not dictating it."

In summary…

Through this chapter, I hope you were able to reflect on factors that may have impacted on your child's ability to access and fully engage in play opportunities and that you understand that it is the coming together of a child and their surrounding play context that either supports or inhibits their ability to access, experience and engage in play. The factors may differ from home to school environments, child to child and family to family. I hope that we, as a society, are able to reflect on the role of adults in nurturing and supporting play, not dictating it.

PAUSE TO PLAY

1. In what ways can you support your little one's free play, such as observing their play interests, providing input in setting the scene, helping them access play prompts, finding a time for free play in their day and/or making a *yes space*?

2. Have you considered additional factors that may impact on free play, such as safety, hunger and connection?

3. Have you considered which skills or area of competence can be accessed with minimal adult guidance to prepare a *yes space* for free play?

4. Have you considered which skills or area of competence can be accessed with adult guidance as part of guided play?

5. Do you currently include more structured activities, guided play or free play? How is time balanced between these? What changes would you like to make?

6. Have you considered your child's current play interests, including play schemas, such as:

- ☐ CONNECTING
- ☐ DISCONNECTING
- ☐ CONTAINING
- ☐ ENVELOPING
- ☐ ENCLOSING
- ☐ TRAJECTORY
- ☐ RADIAL
- ☐ ROTARY
- ☐ BOUNDARIES
- ☐ ORIENTATION
- ☐ ORDERING
- ☐ TRANSFORMING
- ☐ TRANSPORTING
- ☐ ADDITIONAL EG. SOUND

And play themes, such as dinosaurs, nature, space, construction, fairies, animals and so on?

7. Where is your current *yes space* located? Do you want, or need, to make any changes to it (e.g. immediate location, safety considerations, sensory considerations, accessibility and visibility of play prompts, number of play prompts included and so on)?

8. Does your play space allow for:

- ☐ MOVEMENT
- ☐ PRETENSE
- ☐ CONSTRUCTION
- ☐ CREATION
- ☐ REGULATION

9. Are you missing any of the above? What do you want to include more of?

10. What open-ended play prompts do you have in your play space, such as wooden blocks, figurines, cars, dolls, dress up play prompts, balls, play silks or scarves, sand or water toys, boxes and packaging material, art materials and other loose parts?

11. Have you considered the number of open-ended, close-ended and battery-operated toys in the play space?

12. What are some of your child's favourite open-ended play prompts?

13. Which open-ended play prompts does your child play with least?

14. Which strategies are you going to try if your child always wants you to play with (or for) them?

15. What tips do you want to focus on for joining in your child's play?

16. Which strategies are you going to try out if your child can't choose what to play?

17. Which strategies are you going to try to help jump-start from the I'm bored space to play?

18. What were some tips you want to focus on for the *invitation to play* concept?

19. Where and how do you currently display and store play prompts? Does this work for you and your family?

20. Where and how do you present play prompts (e.g. low shelf, child's eye level, baskets or trays)? Does this work for you and your family?

21. Which favourite play prompts do you keep out?

22. If you identify toy rotation as a strategy, which part of the process do you want to focus on more:

☐ COLLECT   ☐ COLLECTIONS

☐ CATEGORISE   ☐ CHOOSE

23. Do you distinguish between hazards and healthy challenges as part of physical (and general) play?

24. Do you consider both environmental and child characteristics when you make a risk analysis? Is there anything you want to try differently in the future?

25. What tips do you want to try out to move away from saying, 'Be careful!' or, 'Watch out!' to build on their ability to risk manage themselves?

"Play is essential for development, foundational to learning and vital to a child's wellbeing. Let us not forget that."

CHAPTER FIVE

PLAY FOR ALL

PLAY FOR ALL

This chapter is by no means extensive. My hope in including a few thoughts on children with varying play needs is to create an awareness for caregivers, parents, teachers, therapists and other health professionals that some children may require more specific input and support to participate and fully engage in play.

There appears to be an overfocus on the child's role as learner or scholar, with little regard for their role as a player, and whether they are able to engage in play to their heart's desire.

Playfulness has been found to remain stable over time if no specific intervention or support is provided to develop this. However, diminished levels of playfulness can improve through targeted intervention, experience and engagement in playful transactions. It may involve a combination of child and environmental interventions. Removing or adapting barriers to play in a child's environment and skilled playful modelling have been found to improve playfulness levels in typically developing children and children with difficulties and disabilities.

Some children with sensory processing disorders, autism spectrum disorder, dyspraxia, physical limitations or impairments, developmental delays, ADHD and other diagnoses may be at risk of being on the side-lines of play engagements, rather than actively participating.

With the various associated benefits of play engagement to a child's development, learning, health and wellbeing, it is critical that more occupational therapists use play assessments and focus on the role of player, as well as that of scholar or learner, for children with varying play needs. I am going to repeat this same sentence from earlier in the book: 'Play deprivation can have a negative impact on physical, cognitive and socio-emotional development'. Key role-players in a child's life should partner together to overcome barriers inhibiting play relevant to each child and their context.

Play is essential for development, foundational to learning and vital to a child's wellbeing. Let us not forget that.

Conclusion

The push towards early writing, literacy and numeracy comes at a significant opportunity cost. Although research studies have demonstrated that earlier is not better, competitive parenting and fear of the future continue to drive this. Play has been deemed less important and less serious than rote learning, structured activities and worksheets. What about creativity, curiosity, critical problem solving, flexible thinking, initiative, grit, adaptability, empathy, being able to negotiate and collaborate with others and leadership? Are these less important or less serious skills?

Play is the vitamins, minerals, fruits and vegetables of childhood. Play is foundational to learning. It forms the building blocks on top of which we later lay scholastic and academic skills. You cannot expect to build a roof on top of toothpicks, yet this is what is happening. As I mentioned in the introduction, children play less than ever before, yet more is expected of them at earlier and earlier ages. Children are not given the time and opportunity to build strong foundations for later scholastic and academic skills. They are expected to jump straight in, without a strong foundation, without a means to keep the roof from collapsing under all the pressure. They are more anxious and more stressed than previous generations.

Early childhood is meant to be filled with magic, discovery and exploration, in other words play. The overfocus on achieving certain scholastic skills when children's bodies and minds are not ready for it takes away the very time and opportunity they need to strengthen and prepare for those very activities and skills that will be part of their schooling for many years to come. Earlier is not better.

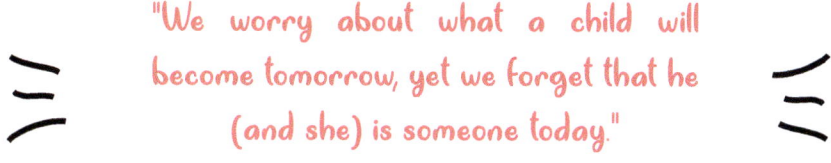

"We worry about what a child will become tomorrow, yet we forget that he (and she) is someone today."

- Stacia Tauscher

To simply state that children should just play more takes away from the significant reality of how we got here in the first place. Yes, my hope and dream is for children to play more, but they need our help and support. It is going to take a conscious effort on our part, the adults' part and society's part, to bring play back to the foreground, to make play accessible, to make play a cherished part of childhood again, to consider the contextual factors that led us here and to make an effort to change those for the better. It requires the coming together of a child and their play context, which includes adults, to support their right to play.

When given the opportunity, space and time, children are wired and internally motivated to explore and learn about themselves and their surrounding world through play. They were born to play. If only we, as adults, can learn to trust in that process once again.

THEY WERE BORN TO PLAY. IF ONLY WE, AS ADULTS, CAN LEARN TO TRUST IN THAT PROCESS ONCE AGAIN.

A few additional acknowledgements

I want to make special mention to Dirkie, Hannah, Andrew, Maré, Matty, Amy, Caitlyn and my family for being on my yes team.

To those who took the time to read and share insights with me along the way. Thank you for the support, especially to Mamma, Ryan, Hannah and Pam.

To Professor Elelwani Ramugondo, Dr Pam Gretschel, Associate Professor Reinie Cordier and our GoKidz research team, which deepened both my love and understanding of the magic that is play.

To Elna Geldenhuys and Jane Durham who have helped shape me as a therapist and allowed me to bring my playful self to their practices.

To Bunty McDougal and Lizahn du Plesis for your advice and support in this new adventure.

To Hannah van der Westhuizen for your speedy assistance and keen eye.

To Kelly - wow you created beauty from that initial word document! Thank you for taking my vision with so much care and creativity and breathing life into it. It has been an exciting journey to see each chapter come alive and I feel fortunate to have your creative genius on my team!

To Jared - thank you for the time, care and detail you put into every line.

To Tertius and his team, thank you for your assistance.

REFERENCES

Alexander, J., Johnson, K., Leibham, M., & Kelley, K. (2008). The Development of Conceptual Interests in Young Children. *Cognitive Development*, (23), 324–334. DOI: 10.1016/j.cogdev.2007.11.004.

American Academy of Pediatrics. (2016). Media and Young Minds: Council on Communications and Media. *Pediatrics*, (138). DOI: http://doi.org/10.1542/peds.2016-2591.

Athey, C. (1990). *Extending thoughts in young children*. London: Paul Chapman Publishing.

Ayres, A. J. (2000). *Sensory Integration and the Child*. Los Angeles: Western Psychological Services.

Bartie, M., Dunnell, A., Kaplan, J., Oosthuizen, D., Smit, D., van Dyk, A., & Duvenage, M. (2015). The Play Experiences of Preschool Children from a Low-socio-economic Rural Community in Worcester, South Africa. *Occupational Therapy International Journal*. 23(2):91-102. DOI: http://doi.org/10.1002/oti.1404.

Bodrova, E., & Leong, D. J. (2007). Play and Early Literacy: A Vygotskian Approach. In: Roskos, K.A. & Christie, J.F. (Eds). Play and Literacy in Early Childhood: Research from Multiple Perspectives, 185–200. 2nd Ed. London: Rouledge

Bodrova, E., Germeroth, C., & Leong, D. J. (2013). Play and Self-Regulation: Lessons from Vygotsky. *American Journal of Play*, (6), 111–123.

Bodrova, E., & Leong, D. J. (2017). Tools of the Mind: A Vygotskian Early Childhood Curriculum. In: Fleer, M., & van Oers, B. International handbook of early childhood education, 1095–1111. Netherlands: Springer.

Bodrova, E. (2008). Make-believe Play Versus Academic Skills: A Vygotskian Approach to Today's Dilemma of Early Childhood Education. *European Early Childhood Education Research Journal*, (16), 357–369.

Brock, A., Jarvis, P., & Olusoga Y. (2019). *Perspectives on Play*. (3rd ed). London: Routledge.

Brown, S. (2010). *Play. How it shapes the brain, opens the imagination and invigorates the soul*. USA: Penguin Books Ltd.

Bruce, T. (2001). *Learning through play*. London: Hodder and Stoughton.

Bundy, A. C., Luckett, T., Naughton, G., Tranter, P. J., Wyver, S. R., Ragen, J., & Spies, G. (2008). Playful Interaction: Occupational Therapy for All Children on the School Playground. *The American Journal of Occupational Therapy*, 62(5), 522–7. DOI: http://doi.org/10.5014/ajot.62.5.522.

Bundy, A. C., Nelson, L., Metzger, M., & Bingaman, K. (2001). Validity and Reliability of a Test of Playfulness. *OTJR: Occupation, Participation and Health*, 21(4), 276–292. DOI: http://doi.org/10.1177/153944920102100405.

Bundy, A.C., Kolrosova, J., Paguinto, S. G., Bray, P., Swain, B., Wallen, M., & Engelen, L. (2011). Comparing the Effectiveness of a Parent Group Intervention with Child-based Intervention for Promoting Playfulness in Children with Disabilities. *The Israeli Journal of Occupational Therapy*, 20(4), 95–113.

Bundy, A.C., Lane, S., & Murray, E. (2002). *Sensory Integration Theory and Practice*. 2nd ed. Philadelphia: F.A. Davis Company.

Bundy, A. C., Naughton, G., Tranter, P., Wyver, S., Baur, L., Schiller, W., Bauman, A., Engelen, L., Ragen, J., Luckett, T., Niehues, A., Stewart, G., Jessup, G., & Brentnall, J. (2011). The Sydney Playground Project: Popping the Bubblewrap – Unleashing the Power of Play: A cluster randomized controlled trial of a primary school playground-based intervention aiming to increase children's physical activity and social skills. *BMC Public Health*, 11(680).

Bundy, A.C., Shia, S., Qi, L. & Miller, L. J. (2007). How does sensory processing dysfunction affect play? *American Journal of Occupational Therapy*, 61, 201-208.

Cantrill, A., Wilkes-Gillan, S., Bundy, A., Cordier, R., & Wilson, N. J. (2015). An eighteen-month follow-up of a pilot parent-delivered play-based intervention to improve the social play skills of children with attention deficit hyperactivity disorder and their playmates. *Australian Occupational Therapy Journal*, 62(3), 197–207. DOI: http://doi.org/10.1111/1440-1630.12203.

Case-Smith, J., & Kuhaneck, H. M. (2008). Play Preferences of Typically Developing Children and Children with Developmental Delays Between Ages 3 and 7 Years. *OTJR: Occupation, Participation & Health*, 28(1), 19–29. DOI: http://doi.org/10.3928/15394492-20080101-01.

Case-Smith, J., & O'Brien, J. C. (2010). *Occupational Therapy for Children*. 6th ed. St Louis, MO: Mosby Elsevier.

Centre on the Developing Child at Harvard University. Resources library: Serve and return (2004–2020). https://developingchild.harvard.edu/resourcetag/serve-and-return/.

Chiarello, L. A., Huntington, A., & Bundy, A. (2006). A comparison of motor behaviors, interaction, and playfulness during mother-child and father-child play with children with motor delay. *Physical & Occupational Therapy in Pediatrics*, 26(1–2), 129–51.

Christakis, D. A., Zimmerman, F. J., DiGiuseppe, D. L., & McCarty, C. A. (2004). Early television exposure and subsequent attentional problems in children. *Pediatrics*, 113(4), 708–713.

Chudacoff, H. P. (2007). *Children at play*. An American History. NY: NYU Press.

Danner, F. W. (2008). A national longitudinal study of the association between hours of TV viewing and the trajectory of BMI growth among US children. *Journal of Pediatric Psychology*, 33(10), 1100–1107. DOI:10.1093/jpepsy/jsn034.

Dauch, C., Imwalle, M., Ocasio, B., & Metz. A. E. (2018). The influence of the number of toys in the environment on toddlers' play. *Infant Behaviour and Development*, 50, 78–87.

Davies, S. (2019). *The Montessori Toddler. A parent's guide to raising a curious and responsible human being*. Workman Publishing: New York

DeLoache, J. S., Chiong, C., Sherman, K., Islam, N., Vanderborght, M., Troseth, G. L., & O'Doherty, K. (2010). Do babies learn from baby media? *Psychological Science*, 21(11), 1570–74. DOI:10.1177/0956797610384145.

DeLoache, J., Simcock, G., & Macari, S. (2007). Planes, Trains, Automobiles- and Tea Sets: Extremely Intense Interests in Very Young Children. *Developmental Psychology*, 43 (15), 79–86. DOI: 10.1037/0012-1649.43.6.1579.

Dunn, W. (1997). The Impact of Sensory Processing Abilities on the Daily Lives of Young Children and Their Families: A Conceptual Model. *Infants & Young Children*, 9(4), 23–35.

Dunn, W. (1999). *The Sensory Profile*. San Antonio, TX: Psychological Corporation.

Dunn, W. (2007). Supporting Children to Participate Successfully in Everyday Life by Using Sensory Processing Knowledge. *Infants & Young Children*, 20(2), 84–101.

Dunn, W. (2014). *The Sensory Profile 2 Manual*. San Antonio, TX: Pearson.

Elkind, D. (2007). *The Power of Play*. Philadelphia: De Capo Press.

Sandseter, E. (2007) Categorising risky play—how can we identify risk-taking in children's play? *European Early Childhood Education Research Journal*, 15(2), 237–252, DOI: 10.1080/13502930701321733.

Engelen, L., Bundy, A. C., Bauman, A., Naughton, G., Wyver, S., & Baur, L. (2015). Young children's after-school activities – There's more to it than screen time: A cross-sectional study of young primary children. *Journal of Physical Activity and Health*, 12(1), 8–12.

Engelen, L., Bundy, A. C., Lau, J., Naughton, G., Wyver, S., Bauman, A., & Baur, L. (2015). Understanding patterns of young children's physical activity after school – It's all about context: A cross-sectional study. *Journal of Physical Activity and Health*, 12(3), 335–339.

Engelen, L., Bundy, A. C., Naughton, G., Jessup, G., & van der Ploeg, H.P. (2013). Preventive Medicine Increasing physical activity in young primary school children - it's child's play: A cluster randomised controlled trial. *Preventive Medicine*, 56(5), 319–325.

Featherstone, S., & Louis, S. (2013). *Understanding Schemas in Young Children*. London: Featherstone Publishers.

Fisher, K. R., Hirsh-Pasek, K., Golinkoff, R. M., & Gryfe, S. G. (2008). Conceptual split? Parents' and experts' perceptions of play in the 21st century. *Journal of Applied Developmental Psychology*, 29(4), 305–316. DOI: http://doi.org/10.1016/j.appdev.2008.04.006.

Gaertner, B. M., Spinrad, T. L., & Eisenberg, N. (2008). Focused attention in toddlers. Measurement, stability, and relations to negative emotion and parenting. *Infant Child Development*, 17(4), 339–363.

Ginsburg, K. R. (2007). The importance of play in promoting healthy child development and maintaining strong parent-child bonds. *Pediatrics*, 119(1), 182–191. DOI: http://doi.org/10.1542/peds.2011-2953.

Goldschmied, E., & Jackson, S. (2004). *People under Three, Young Children in Day Care*. 3rd Ed. London: Routledge.

Gordon, G. (2014). Well Played: The Origins and Future of Playfulness. *American Journal of Play*, 6(2), 234–266.

Gray, P. (2013). *Free to learn*. New York: Basic Books.

Hale, L., & Guan, S. (2015). Screen time and sleep among school-aged children and adolescents: A systematic literature review. *Sleep Medicine Reviews*, 21, 50–58. DOI: 10.1016/j.smrv.2014.07.007.

Hebb, D.O. (1961). Distinctive Features of Learning in the Higher Animal. In J.F. Delafresnaye (Ed.), *Brain Mechanisms and Learning*. 37–46. Oxford: Blackwell.

Hirsh-Pasek, K., & Golinkoff, R. H. (2003). *Einstein Never Used Flash Cards*. USA: Rodale Books.

Jarvis, P. (2006). Rough and tumble play: Lessons in life. *Evolutionary Psychology*, 4, 330–346.

Jarvis, P. (2007). Monsters, magic and Mr. Psycho: A biocultural approach to rough and tumble play in the early years of primary school. *Early Years: An International Journal of Research and Development*, 27(2), 171–188.

Jensen, H., Pyle, A., Alaca, B., & Fesseha, E. (2019). Playing with a goal in mind: exploring the enactment of guided play in Canadian and South African early years classrooms. *Early Years*. DOI: 10.1080/09575146.2019.1619670

Kent, C., Cordier, R., Joosten, A.V., Wilkes-Gillan, S., Bundy, A., & Speyer, R. (2020). A Systematic Review and Meta-analysis of Interventions to Improve Play Skills in Children with Autism Spectrum Disorder. *Review Journal of Autism and Developmental Disorders*, 7(7), 91–118. DOI: https://doi.org/10.1007/s40489-019-00181-y.

Knox, S. (2008). Development and current use of the Revised Knox Preschool Play Scale. In Parham, L. L., & Fazio, L. S. (Eds). *Play in Occupational Therapy for Children*, 55–70. 2nd Ed. USA: Mosby Elsevier.

Lansbury, J. (2014). *Elevating Child Care. A guide to respectful parenting*. USA: JLML Press.

Leong, D. J., & Bodrova, E. (2012). Assessing and Scaffolding Make-Believe Play. *Young Children*, (67), 28–34.

Madigan, S., Browne, D., Racine, N., Mori, C., & Tough, S. (2019). Association between Screen Time and Children's Performance on a Developmental Screening Test. *JAMA Pediatrics*, 173(3), 244–250. DOI: https://doi.org/10.1001/jamapediatrics.2018.5056.

McClintic, S., & Petty, K. (2015). Exploring Early Childhood Teachers' Beliefs and Practices About Preschool Outdoor Play: A Qualitative Study. *Journal of Early Childhood Teacher Education*, 36(1), 24–43. DOI: http://doi.org/10.1080/10901027.2014.997844.

Murphy, L. (2016). Lisa Murphy on Play: *The Foundation of Children's Learning*. St Paul: Redleaf Press.

Nutbrown, C. (1999). *Threads of thinking*. London: Paul Chapman Publishing Ltd

O'Brien, J., & Shirley, R. J. (2001). Does playfulness change over time? A preliminary look using the Test of Playfulness. *Occupational Therapy Journal of Research*, 21(2), 132–139.

O'Brien, J., Coker, P., Lynn, R., Suppinger, R., Pearigen, T., Rabon, S. & Ward, A. T. (2000). The Impact of Occupational Therapy on a Child's Playfulness. *Occupational Therapy in Health Care*, 12(2/3), 39–51. http://doi.org/10.1300/J003v12n02_03

Okimoto, M., Bundy, A., & Hanzlik, J. (2000). Playfulness in children with and without disability: measurement and intervention. *The American Journal of Occupational Therapy*, 54(1), 73–82. DOI: http://www.ncbi.nlm.nih.gov/pubmed/10686630.

Parham, L. D. (2008). Play and occupational therapy. In Parham L. D., & Fazio L. S. (Eds.). *Play in occupational therapy for children*, 3–39. (2nd Ed). USA: Moseby Elsevier

Parten, M. B. (1932). Social participation among pre-school children. The Journal of Abnormal and Social Psychology, 27(3), 243–269. DOI: https://doi.org/10.1037/h0074524.
Piaget, J., & Cook, M. T. (1952). *The origins of intelligence in children*. New York: International University Press.

Pyle, A., & Danniels, E. (2017). A Continuum of Play-Based Learning: The Role of the Teacher in Play-Based Pedagogy and the Fear of Hijacking Play. *Early Education and Development*, 28(3), 274–289. DOI: 10.1080/10409289.2016.1220771.

Radesky, J. S., Peacock-Chambers, E., & Zuckerman, B. (2016). Use of mobile technology to calm upset children: Associations with social-emotional development. *JAMA Pediatrics*, 170(4), 397–9.

Ramugondo, E., Ferreira, A., Chung, D., & Cordier, R. (2018). A Feasibility RCT Evaluating a Play-Informed, Caregiver-Implemented, Home-Based Intervention to Improve the Play of Children Who Are HIV Positive. *Occupational Therapy International*. DOI: https://doi.org/10.1155/2018/3652529.

Ruff, H. A., & Capozzoli, M. C. (2003). Development of attention and distractibility in the first 4 years of life. *Developmental Psychology*, 39(5), 877–890.

Sandsetter, E. (2007). Categorizing Risky Play - How can we identify risk-taking in children's play? *European Early Childhood Education Research Journal*, 15(2), 237–52.

Sandsetter, E. (2009). Characteristics of Risky Play. *Journal of Adventure Education & Outdoor Learning*, 9(1), 3–21.

Sandsetter, E. (2009). Children's Expressions of Exhilaration and Fear in Risky Play. *Contemporary Issues in Early Childhood*, 10(2), 92–106.

Sandsetter, E., & Leif E. (2011). Children's Risky Play from an Evolutionary Perspective: The Anti-Phobic Effects of Thrilling Experiences. *Evolutionary Psychology*, 9(2), 257–84.

Singer, D. G., Singer, J. L., Agostino, H. D., & Delong, R. (2009). Children's Pastimes and Play in Sixteen Nations Is Free-Play Declining? *American Journal of Play*, 1(3), 283–312.

Skaines, N., Rodger, S., & Bundy, A. (2006). Playfulness in Children with Autistic Disorder and their Typically Developing Peers. *British Journal of Occupational Therapy*, 69(11), 505–512.

Skard, G., & Bundy, A. C. (2008). Test of Playfulness. In Parham, L. L. & Fazio L. S., *Play in Occupational Therapy for Children*, 71–93. (2nd Ed). USA: Moseby Elsevier.

Stagnitti, K. (2004). Understanding play: The implications for play assessment. *Australian Occupational Therapy Journal*, 51(1), 3–12.

Steiner-Adair, C. (2013). *The Big Disconnect.* NY: Harper Collins Publishers.

Sutton-Smith, B. (1997) *The ambiguity of play.* USA: Harvard University Press: London.

Takata, N. (1974). Play as a prescription. In Reilly, M. (Ed). *Play as Exploratory Learning*, 209–46. Beverly Hills, CA: Sage Publications.

Twenge, J. M., Campbell, W. K. (2018). Associations between screen time and lower psychological well-being among children and adolescents: Evidence from a population-based study. *Preventative Medicine Reports*, 18(12), 271–83. DOI: 10.1016/j.pmedr.2018.10.003.

Uys, A. (2016). *A randomized control trial investigating the effect of a play-informed caregiver-implemented home-based intervention on playfulness for HIV positive children aged 10 months to 8 years on HAART from a low socio-economic status* (Master's Thesis). University of Cape Town, Cape Town, South Africa.

Vigil, K. B. (2019). Portable screen time and kindergarteners' attention with content as a potential moderator. *Frontiers in Education Technology.* 2(3), 141-158. DOI: 10.22158/fet.v2n3p141.

Vygotsky, L. (1986). *Thought and Language.* USA: MIT Press.

Vygotsky, L.S. (1977). Play and Its Role in the Mental Development of the Child. *Soviet Developmental Psychology*, 76–99.

Walsh, J. J., Barnes, J. D., Cameron, D. C., Goldfield, G. S., Chaput, J., Gunnell, K., Ledoux, A., Zemek, R. L., Tremblay, M. S. (2018). Associations between 24 hour movement behaviours and global cognition in US children: a cross-sectional observational study. *The Lancet. Child and Adolescent Health*, 2(11), 783–91. DOI: https://doi.org/10.1016/S2352-4642(18)30278-5.

Weisberg, D. S, Hirsh-Pasek, K., Golinkoff, R. M., Kittredge, A. K., & Klahr, D. (2016). Guided Play: Principles and Practices. *Current Directions in Psychological Science*, 25(3), 177–82.

WHO guidelines on physical activity, sedentary behaviour and sleep for children under 5 years of age. (2019). Geneva: World Health Organization. Licence: CC BY-NC-SA 3.0 IGO.

Wilkes, S., Cordier, R., Bundy, A., Docking, K., & Munro, N. (2011). A play-based intervention for children with ADHD: a pilot study. *Australian Occupational Therapy Journal*, 58(4), 231–40. DOI: http://doi.org/10.1111/j.1440-1630.2011.00928.x.

Wilkes-Gillan, S., Bundy, A., Cordier, R., & Lincoln, M. (2014). Evaluation of a Pilot Parent-Delivered Play-Based Intervention for Children with Attention Deficit Hyperactivity Disorder, 68(6), 700–9. *The American Journal of Occupational Therapy.* DOI: http://doi.org/http://dx.doi.org/10.5014/ajot.2014.012450.

Wyver, S., Tranter, P., Naughton, G., Little, H., Sandseter, E., & Bundy, A. (2010). Ten ways to restrict children's freedom to play: The problem of surplus safety. *Contemporary Issues in Early Childhood*, 11(3), 263–77.

Yogman, M., Garner, A., Hutchinson, J., Hirsh-Pasek, K., & Golinkoff, R.M. (2018). The Power of Play: A Pediatric Role in Enhancing Development in Young Children. *American Academy of Pediatrics: Pediatrics*,.142(3), 1–16. DOI: 10.1542/peds.2018-2058.

Youell, B. (2008). The importance of play and playfulness. *European Journal of Psychotherapy & Counselling*, 10(2), 121–129. http://doi.org/10.1080/13642530802076193.

Zhao, J., Zhang, Y., Jiang, F., Ip, F., Ka Wing Ho, F., Zhang, Y., & Huang, H. (2018) Excessive Screen Time and Psychosocial Well-Being: The Mediating Role of Body Mass Index, Sleep Duration, and Parent-Child Interaction. *The Journal of Pediatrics*. 202, 157-162. DOI: 10.1016/j.jpeds.2018.06.029.

www.ingramcontent.com/pod-product-compliance
Lightning Source LLC
Chambersburg PA
CBHW061749290426

44108CB00028B/2931